Stochastic and Tree-Based Machine Learning for Air Pollution Forecasting

nova science publishers
www.novapublishers.com
New York

Computer Science, Technology and Applications Series

The Deepfake Dilemma: Safeguarding Institutions and Citizens in the Digital Age
Ruben Faulkner (Editor)
ISBN: 979-8-90134-122-3
eBook ISBN: 979-8-90134-143-8

Unleashing Machine Learning for Advanced Threat Detection and Prevention in Industry 4.0
Mehak Khurana, PhD,
Shilpa Mahajan, PhD,
and Asif Ali Laghari, PhD
ISBN: 979-8-90134-061-5
eBook ISBN: 979-8-90134-115-5

Cybersecurity Challenges and Strategies Across Sectors and Government Agencies
Marybeth Wiskoff (Editor)
ISBN: 979-8-90134-039-4
eBook ISBN: 979-8-90134-065-3

Building Intelligent Systems for the Future: Mastering the Revolution in Cognitive Computing
Anamika Ahirwar, PhD,
Neelesh Jain, PhD,
and Sumitha Elayaperumal, PhD
ISBN: 979-8-90134-050-9
eBook ISBN: 979-8-90134-094-3

Smart Decision Systems: Integrating Symbolic AI and Cognitive Heuristics for IOMT
Hemant Kumar Saini, PhD,
Christian Kaunert
and Bhupinder Singh
ISBN: 979-8-89530-935-3
eBook ISBN: 979-8-89530-993-3

More information about this series can be found at

Snezhana Gocheva-Ilieva
Atanas Ivanov
Maya Stoimenova-Minova

Stochastic and Tree-Based Machine Learning for Air Pollution Forecasting

nova
science publishers
www.novapublishers.com
New York

DOI: https://doi.org/10.52305/ZGUC4344

Additional color graphics may be available in the e-book version of this book.

Library of Congress Cataloging-in-Publication Data

ISBN: 979-8-90134-206-0 (Softcover)
ISBN: 979-8-90134-285-5 (eBook)

Published by Nova Science Publishers, Inc. † New York

To my husband Iliycho, my sons Georgi and Neven, my daughter-in-law Gergana, and my lovely granddaughters Mihaela and Sofya

Snezhana Gocheva-Ilieva, Professor, DSc, PhD

To my wife, in sincere appreciation of her constant support, and to our three wonderful children, whose presence enriches my life and gives purpose to my work

Atanas Ivanov, Associate Professor, PhD

To my dear family: my husband Ivan, who supports me unconditionally, my parents, and my brother

Maya Stoimenova-Minova, PhD

Contents

Preface

Machine learning (ML) is a basic paradigm of artificial intelligence, also called the "ultimate statistician" of our time [1]. Its roots date back to 1943, when Walter Pitts and Warren McCulloch first published neural network algorithms for mathematical modeling of biological neurons [2]. Later, in 1959, Arthur Samuel introduced the term machine learning in his seminal paper describing in detail a computer program that demonstrated that the computer could be programmed to outplay its programmer [1, 3]. Another, more straightforward definition describes ML as "the combination of automated computer algorithms with powerful statistical methods to learn hidden patterns in rich datasets. In that sense, Statistical Learning Theory gives the statistical foundation of ML" [4].

In the modern world, ML is a powerful tool for processing data through modeling, experimentation and simulated study of various phenomena and processes, for testing theories in practice, making predictions, and taking management decisions, etc. ML is applied together with the apparatus of traditional statistics in all spheres of life and enables the extraction of essential information from the accumulated large datasets. As a result, the cost and time for design, analysis, and forecasting are significantly reduced, and skilled human labor is saved.

This book uses some ML methods for modeling and forecasting data from measurements of various air pollutants. Observed real variables are random in nature, being influenced by a large number of known and unknown random factors. Therefore, from a statistical point of view, they are classified as stochastic processes. For their modeling, we will also apply appropriate stochastic modeling methods. From the many different definitions of the term "stochastic process" presented in the literature, by this term we will understand any collection of random variables defined on a common probability space, taking values in a common "state space," and indexed by the continuous-time parameter [5]. Simply put, a stochastic process is a continuous-time analogue of a random sequence, and the considered datasets are their discrete representation in the form of time series with measured values.

The results presented in this book are partially based on several recent publications of the authors from the period 2020-2024 [6-14]. The purpose of the conducted research is to study, analyze and forecast the air quality in urban areas. A second goal is to research the most appropriate methods for forecasting and evaluating the influence of various meteorological and atmospheric factors on the concentration of harmful emissions.

In the last few years, there has been a growing number of publications of new models in this area, which seek to include as many variables as possible determining pollution levels, as well as models for large geographical areas and even entire countries (see, for instance, [15, 16]).

In contrast to them, most of our study relies on models that are as parsimonious as possible, with fewer variables and/or less data for individual cities. This makes it possible to obtain more accurate short-term forecasts, since the data themselves implicitly (i.e., stochastically) take into account their local nature - climate, landscape, anthropogenic sources (transport, enterprises emitting harmful pollutants and others). On the other hand, such type of local economic models requires smaller computational resources (memory, machine time, data transfer rate, etc.). Therefore, they are more suitable for implementation, including in mobile applications and distributed networks for providing real-time information to public use.

The developed ML models and statistical approaches study the concentrations of various air pollutants, including particulate matter (PM) of different sizes, from 10, 2.5, and 1 micron - PM_{10}, $PM_{2.5}$, and PM_1, SO_2, NO_2, CO_2, and others. Among them, the pollutant PM_{10} is the most problematic for the selected cities in Bulgaria. All data used are from official sources.

Chapter 1 of this book provides an overview of air pollutants and their adverse health effects, the importance of emissions modeling, and a literature review of the current state of scientific publications in this area. Chapter 2 contains basic concepts of time series and raw data pre-processing. The stages of data pre-processing include descriptive statistics, examination of the statistical distribution of data, data transformations, filling in missing data, autocorrelation and partial autocorrelation functions (ACF and PACF), principal component analysis (PCA), factor analysis, some authors' algorithms, statistical tests, and other approaches. They are accordingly described briefly in Chapter 2, as well as in the relevant subsequent analyses.

Chapter 3 describes the conceptual foundations of the methods used throughout the book. Their applications are further presented in the next five chapters as case studies of real-world data from measurements in different Bulgarian cities.

A number of empirical predictive models of air pollutants have been built and analyzed. Modeling is of a regression type. It was conducted with over 10 types of different methods and approaches. The classical methods include the parametric stochastic method of Autoregressive Integrated Moving Average (ARIMA) and its variants - seasonal ARIMA (SARIMA), ARIMA with Transfer Functions (ARIMA/TF), as well as Granger causality for time series, and others. Different variants of the discrete wavelet transform (DWT) are used for trend extraction and data denoising, including the selection of an adaptive threshold for the inverse transformation.

ML models are built with decision tree methods, where the trees are generated by applying the Classification and Regression Trees (CART) algorithm [17, 18]. Individual models are built using CART or Random Forests (RF) methods and/or their hybridization by means of ARIMA in Chapters 4 and 5, respectively. The main results in this book are based on ensembles of decision trees. In the following chapters of the book, high-performance ML models with high statistical indicators and perfect forecasting results are obtained with RF, CART Ensembles and Bagging (CART EBag), Adaptively resampling and combine (Arcing, or Arc-x4). With some of these methods, new hybrid and stacked models have also been developed, and it has been demonstrated that the latter two types of models exceed the accuracy of their base models.

The selection of a model and the assessment of all models was performed through statistical tests, rigorous residual diagnostic checks, and application of a variety of statistical measures of accuracy and goodness of fit, such as root mean squared error (RMSE), mean absolute percentage error (MAPE), coefficient of determination R^2, Willmott coefficient of agreement, and more. Some information criteria were also used, such as the Bayesian information criterion.

We will note some main contributions of the results presented in this book. In general, results with ensemble learning using CART-EBag and Arcing in the literature are episodic, and in particular, their ability to predict and analyze time series with rapidly changing data in ecology, of the type we modeled, has not been sufficiently explored. In several of our studies on independent datasets, we have demonstrated that these two methods have very good qualities for time-series analysis and forecasting, with Arcing models outperforming RF in many cases.

Another contribution is the development and implementation of the author's hybrid type algorithms, which provides an additional option to ML strategies. In the area of the stacking paradigm, we demonstrate flexible ways to combine stacked wavelets with a stacked modeling approach.

An important point in the presented case studies is not only obtaining high-performance models based on a small number of predictors. In order to achieve statistical adequacy and good short-term forecasts, it is constantly demonstrated how to examine model errors for effective reliability and inference from the built models.

We believe that this monograph will be useful for researchers, PhD students, and all those interested in modern data processing methods, not only in the field of environmental studies, but also in other areas of data science.

Snezhana Gocheva-Ilieva,
Professor, Dr, DSc,
Plovdiv University "Paisii Hilendarski," Bulgaria

,
Associate Professor, Dr,
Plovdiv University "Paisii Hilendarski," Bulgaria

Maya Stoimenova-Minova,
Assistant Professor, Dr,
Plovdiv University "Paisii Hilendarski," Bulgaria

Financing:

This monograph has emanated from research conducted with the financial support of the Bulgarian National Science Fund (BNSF) under the Grant No. KP-06-IP-CHINA/1 (КП-06-ИП-КИТАЙ/1).

References

[1] Karjian, J., 2023. *History and evolution of machine learning: A timeline*. WhatIs, September, 22. https://www.techtarget.com/whatis/A-Timeline-of-Machine-Learning-History.

[2] McCulloch, W. S. and Pitts, W., 1943. A logical calculus of the ideas immanent in nervous activity. *Bulletin of Mathematical Biophysics*, 5, pp. 115-133.

[3] Samuel, A. L, 1959. Some studies in machine learning using the game of checkers. *IBM Journal of Research and Development*, 3(3). (Reprint: IBM Journal of Research and Development, 44(1.2), 206-226, 2000. http://doi.org/10.1147/rd.441.0206).

[4] Masini, R. P., Medeiros, M. C. and Mendes, E. F., 2023. Machine learning advances for time series forecasting. *Journal of Economic Surveys*, 37(1), pp. 76-111.

[5] Fristedt, B. E. and Gray, L. F., 1997. *A Modern Approach to Probability Theory*. Birkhäuser, p. 580.

[6] Gocheva-Ilieva, S., Ivanov, A. and Stoimenova-Minova, M., 2020. Prediction of PM10 air pollution using random forests with ARIMA error correction. In *19th Conference on Applied Mathematics (APLIMAT 2020), Aplimat Conference Proceedings*, Slovak University of Technology in Bratislava, Bratislava, pp. 537-545, POD Publ: Curran Associates, Inc.

[7] Stoimenova-Minova, M. P., Gocheva-Ilieva, S. G. and Ivanov, A. V., 2020, June. PM10 prediction using CART method depending on the number of observations. In *Proceedings of the 2020 3rd International Conference on Mathematics and Statistics (ICoMS), ACM International Conference Proceedings Series* (ICPS), (pp. 65-70).

[8] Ivanov, A., Gocheva-Ilieva, S. and Stoimenova, M., 2020, December. Hybrid boosted trees and regularized regression for studying ground ozone and PM10 concentrations. In *AIP Conference Proceedings* (Vol. 2302, No. 1). AIP Publishing.

[9] Ivanov, A., Gocheva-Ilieva, S. and Stoimenova-Minova, M., 2022, September. Random forest regression for statistical modeling and forecasting of PM10. In *AIP Conference Proceedings* (Vol. 2522, No. 1). AIP Publishing.

[10] Gocheva-Ilieva, S. G., Ivanov, A. V. and Stoimenova-Minova, M. P., 2022. Prediction of daily mean PM10 concentrations using random forest and CART ensemble and bagging stacked by MARS. *Sustainability*, 14(2), art. 798.

[11] Gocheva-Ilieva S. G., Ivanov A. V., Kulina, H. N. and Stoimenova-Minova M. P., 2023. Multi-step ahead ex ante forecasting of air pollutants using machine learning. *Mathematics*, 11 (7), art. 566. https://doi.org/10.3390/math11071566.

[12] Ivanov, A. V., Gocheva-Ilieva, S. G. and Stoimenova-Minova, M. P., 2023, December. Temporal-causal modeling of air pollution in the city of Plovdiv, Bulgaria: a case study. In *Journal of Physics: Conference Series* (Vol. 2675, No. 1, p. 012002). IOP Publishing.

[13] Gocheva-Ilieva, S. G., Ivanov, A. V., Stoimenova-Minova, M. P. and Koleva-Pavlova, S. K., 2023. Discrete wavelet transform and ensemble tree algorithms for air pollutant modeling: A case study. *International Journal of Membrane Science and Technology*, 10(4), 1357-1373.

[14] Stoimenova-Minova, M., Gocheva-Ilieva, S. and Ivanov, A., 2023, July. Application of Discrete Wavelet Transform and Tree-Based Ensemble Machine Learning for Modeling of Particulate Matter Concentrations. In *International Conference on Mathematics and its Applications in Science and Engineering* (pp. 171-183). Cham: Springer Nature Switzerland.

[15] Xu, X., Hao, J., Liang, Y. and Shen, J., 2024. Assessing the nonlinear relationship between land cover change and PM10 concentration change in China. *Land*, 13(6), art.766.

[16] Li, Y., Liu, M., Lv, L., Liang, J., Ma, M., Liu, M. and Fu, P., 2024. Quantitative analysis of spatiotemporal patterns and factor contributions of surface ozone in the North China plain. *Applied Sciences*, 14(12), art. 5026.

[17] Breiman, L., Friedman, J. H., Stone, C. J. and Olshen, R. A., 1984. *Classification and Regression Trees.* Chapman & Hall Wadsworth, Inc., New York.

[18] Steinberg, D., 2009. *CART: Classification and Regression Trees. In The Top Ten Algorithms in Data Mining* (pp. 179-202). Chapman and Hall/CRC.

Chapter 1

Environmental Issues in Air Pollution Modeling

Abstract

Air pollution with aerosols. harmful to health and the environment. is a key problem of the modern world. This book is devoted to the modeling of time series-data with measured concentrations of major urban air pollutants and related meteorological, atmospheric, and other rapidly changing variables. The goal is, through stochastic and modern intelligent machine learning (ML) methods and algorithms, to extract, analyze, and explain the essential relationships between them, to identify the main variables (factors) that influence pollution levels, and to demonstrate the generation of short-term forecasts of future pollution. This chapter presents the main steps and requirements for statistical modeling with ML, the application area, and a literature review on the topic.

Keywords: air pollution, air pollutant, forecasting, ensemble, machine learning (ML), meteorological predictors, predictive model, time series

1.1. Time Series Modeling

The time series we consider are characterized by strong variability, possible long-term internal dependencies (trends), cyclical behavior, the presence of extreme values - jumps, called outliers, and other features. One way to discover interrelationships, dependencies, and characteristic patterns in this type of empirical data is statistical modeling. In essence, it is an iterative building process involving the creation, analysis, evaluation, and implementation of statistical models. Statistical models are widely applied in all fields of science and practice - from natural sciences - physics, chemistry, biology, medicine, engineering sciences, etc., to social sciences - economics, sociology, political science, and more. Statistical modeling is used when the initial system or process exhibits stochastic behavior and can be described by random variables and random functions.

The main classes of machine learning (ML) methods for statistical modelling are artificial neural networks (ANN), Decision trees, Support Vector Machine (SVM), hybrid methods, etc. In modelling procedures, it is important to respect the relevant theoretical assumptions, perform the necessary statistical evaluations and statistical hypothesis tests confirming the model's inference. Unfortunately, in recent times, many authors do not comply with the scientific requirements for reliability of the analyses and present results obtained only with intensive calculations, without observing the statistical theory. This type of results cannot be taken as reliable.

When modeling empirical data, two main types of problems are usually solved - classification and regression. Classification (of variables or observations) is applied when looking for common features and patterns in a dataset to identify groupings along some given attribute, to identify coincidence and strong multicollinearity, and more. On the other hand, the regression model examines the relationships between variables, with one or more of which are dependent variables (targets) and the others are independent variables (predictors, factors). Regression analysis is often used to determine the extent to which the independent variables influence the dependent variable(s) so that the model can predict future values of the dependent variables, etc. ML is the most powerful modern computing tool that provides numerous highly efficient methods and algorithms for solving classification and regression problems for small and large datasets with complex characteristics and relationships.

The first stage in data modeling is the statement of the problem and determination of the research objectives. An independent cyclic process of modeling is started with a procedure for initial planning and conducting experiments for collecting empirical data or collecting and initial processing of so-called historical data from already existing databases or other sources. At the next stage, the type, values, and other characteristics of the individual variables are determined from the initial data. The next and most essential stage is the construction of an adequate and accurate model. In our case, one or more regression ML models are built, which, after being "trained" on a part of the given dataset, are evaluated and used to predict the values of the test dataset, considered as "new data." During training, a learning algorithm iteratively adjusts the model's hyperparameters to minimize some predefined loss function and predictive error.

Traditional modeling is considered model-driven, which is performed with numerical algorithms and models, and the overall type of the regression dependence sought is set with equations and systems of equations - algebraic, differential, integro-differential, etc., with the relevant conditions and parameters. In contrast, the ML approach is data-driven and highly dependent on the specific data. Another major difference is that ML models are trained on a chosen strategy by training on a part of the data and validated on another part of the data that is not used in the modeling procedure. Thus, the model "tests" and improves its capabilities for modeling new "unseen data," which is at the heart of the artificial intelligence (AI) paradigm. The process of modeling with ML requires an initial setting of the hyperparameters of the algorithms used. It is done manually, semi-automatically, or automatically. Modelling with ML includes variable selection from the available pool of time series data, model building, and selection of the best model(s).

A tricky step in ML is model selection. Here we should mention George Box's famous aphorism that "All models are wrong, but some are useful" [1]. The model cannot exactly fit the original observed data, and so its error must be controlled. Statistical measures of bias and variance are usually considered in model selection, but model performance is also often a more important issue, i.e., its characteristics for its accuracy in predicting the test sample. The following three metrics for evaluating the trained regression model are often used: variance, bias, and error. In the case of time series, a very important step is to check for serial correlation in residuals.

Additionally, various criteria for selecting the best model have been developed in the literature. The most frequently used criteria are the cross-validation (CV), Akaike criterion, Schwartz criterion, Hannan-Quinn criterion, Watanabe-Akaike information criterion, and others [2-4]. They apply to nested models when only the number of model parameters is initially changed, not the method by which they are generated. Finally, we can generalize the difficult problem of ML model selection with Wolpert and Macready's No Free Lunch (NFL) theorem [5], which rigorously proves that there is no single best algorithm for all problems.

1.2. Field of Application: Atmospheric Air Pollution

One of the most acute and topical problems of the modern world is environmental protection. An important part of the Earth's overall threatened environment is its atmosphere, and in particular, air pollution in urban areas.

Research in this field refers to environmental science. It is a multidisciplinary scientific field bringing together elements of physics, chemistry, biology, atmospheric sciences, geology, oceanography, etc. Mathematics, computer science, and communication and information technologies find important applications here.

1.2.1. Air Pollutants

Air pollutant emissions in the atmosphere are the principal drivers behind outdoor air pollution. Air pollutants are primary and secondary. Primary pollutants are spread directly into the atmosphere, while secondary pollutants are released as a result of various chemical reactions and processes from primary pollutants, aerosols, and other substances in the atmosphere. Air pollutants are of natural, anthropogenic, or mixed origin according to their sources. The main primary air pollutants are particulate matter (PM), sulfur dioxide (SO_2), nitrogen oxides (NOx), nitrogen dioxide (NO_2), and others. Secondary air pollutants are some PM, tropospheric ozone O_3, and some oxidized volatile organic compounds (VOCs). In particular, precursor gases for the secondary PM are SO_2, NOx, ammonia (NH_3) and VOCs. The other main secondary pollutant is ozone O_3. It is formed in the atmosphere during sunlight from chemical reactions in the presence of NOx, carbon monoxide (CO), VOCs and methane (CH_4).

Main pollutants are:

- Particulate matter (PM)

PM is a common proxy indicator for air pollution. PM are solid and liquid particles suspended in the air. They include various-sized particles containing sulfates, nitrates, ammonia, sodium chloride, black carbon, mineral dust, water and others. Three levels of PM are measured: PM_{10} – particles less than $10\mu m$, $PM_{2.5}$ – particles less than $2.5\mu m$ and PM_1 – particles less than $1\mu m$.

- Nitrogen dioxide (NO_2)

NO_2 is a gaseous air pollutant with a red-brown color, related to NOx. Concentrations of NO_2 are released into the atmosphere by burning fuels at high temperatures in the transport and industrial sectors.

- Sulfur dioxide (SO_2)

SO_2 is a toxic, colorless gas that can be recognized by its pungent smell. It enters the atmosphere as a result of various combustion processes, such as the burning of fossil fuels (coal, oil) and heat treatment of mineral ores that contain sulfur.

- Carbon dioxide (CO_2)

CO_2 is a toxic and dangerous gas, colorless, odorless, and tasteless. It is produced by the incomplete combustion of carbonaceous fuels such as petrol, charcoal, wood, natural gas, and kerosene.

- Ground-level ozone (O_3)

The ground-level ozone O_3 (tropospheric ozone) is a secondary air pollutant. It is a colorless gas that forms in the layers close to the ground. It is formed in sunlight through chemical reactions of other gases. O_3 is a major part of photochemical smog.

Systematized information on key air pollutants and standards for the European Union (EU) is given in Table 1.1 (see also [6-8]).

Ambient air quality does not depend only on emissions and the spread of pollutants from human activity, but is also affected by many other factors, including:

- proximity to the source of harmful emissions;
- local weather conditions, including air temperature, wind strength and direction, sunshine, and others;
- the chemical reactions and interactions between different gases and suspensions in the air;
- local geographical features such as climate, landscape, nearby large bodies of water, transport facilities and others.

To reduce harmful emissions and improve air quality, special preventive measures and laws are implemented in many countries around the world. In the member states of the European Union, uniform standards and measures have been introduced for monitoring, control, and prevention of air pollution from the main air pollutants: SO_2, NOx, NO_2, CO, PM_{10}, $PM_{2.5}$, and O_3 [7].

The current status of EU states is published in a recent air quality report [9]. During the last 10 years, Bulgaria has been continuously ranked poorly in these reports as one of the member states with the highest air pollution by PM_{10}. This process has not been overcome and remains critical for a large number of Bulgarian cities, such as the capital Sofia, Plovdiv, Burgas, and more.

Table 1.1. Air pollutants sources and EU norms

Pollutant	Major sources	EU norms	
		Upper threshold value and period	Limits[a]
PM_{10}	Combustion and non-combustion sources, combustion processes in industry and households, soil and road dust, waste treatment, sea spray, agricultural tilling, transport, sea salt, Saharan dust, atmospheric nucleation	$50\ \mu g/m^3$ per day $40\ \mu g/m^3$ per year	35
$PM_{2.5}$	As with PM_{10}	$20\ \mu g/m^3$ per year	-
SO_2	Fossil fuel combustion, household coal burning, natural emissions	$350\ \mu g/m^3$ per hour, $125\ \mu g/m^3$ per day	24 3
NOx, NO, NO_2	Fuel combustion from industry, road transport, microbial activity in soils, biomass burning	$200\ \mu g/m^3$ per hour, $40\ \mu g/m^3$ per year	18
CO	On-road transportation from gasoline- or diesel-powered engines, off-road engines, biomass burning	$10\ \mu g/m^3$, max daily 8-hour mean	-
CO_2	Fossil fuels, production of cement, forest fires, other natural sources	Without regulation	
O_3	Generated from NO, NO_2, CO, VOCs, methane (CH_4), and natural processes in stratosphere	$20\ \mu g/m^3$, max daily 8-hour mean	25 days over 3 years

[a] Permitted exceedances each year.

We will note that despite the imposed measures to reduce emissions of all harmful pollutants, they are still less strict than the World Health Organization (WHO) guidelines [10]. Monitoring and control in the EU countries are carried out by the European Environment Agency (EEA) [11]. Within the framework of the implemented measures, an online system for informing the population was developed, namely the European Air Quality Index (EAQI) [12]. It enables the retrieval of the current state of air quality in European cities, with up to a 3-hour delay, as well as the provision of forecasts.

The EAQI includes 5 main pollutants – PM_{10}, $PM_{2.5}$, NO_2, O_3 and SO_2. The policy of all EU countries, to one degree or another, is aimed at actively monitoring the key indicators of pollution in certain parts of their territory. In Bulgaria, as a member state of the European Union, 12 key indicators of atmospheric air pollution are systematically monitored at over 36 automatic stations managed by the Executive Environment Agency (ExEA), Bulgaria [13]. Monitoring is carried out in accordance with European directives and air quality standards. Regular reports on ambient air quality are prepared for all regions of the country. Even though the last 5 years have seen a good reduction of harmful pollution, it is still above prescribed limits in many cities. Further improvement requires continued monitoring and careful study of the state of air quality in order to achieve sustainable development and a healthy urban atmosphere.

1.2.2. Health Impacts of Air Pollution

Air quality in urbanized areas is an essential element of the environment, with a direct impact on human health. Key facts about ambient (outdoor) air pollution and health are outlined by the World Health Organization [14]. This bulletin reports that the effects of ambient air pollution are associated with 4.2 million premature deaths worldwide per year in 2019. From these, WHO estimated that some 37% were due to ischemic heart disease and stroke, 18% and 23% of deaths were due to chronic obstructive pulmonary disease and acute lower respiratory infections, respectively, and 11% of deaths were due to cancer within the respiratory tract. Health impacts of air pollution and the current situation in Europe could be found in [15] (see also Figure 1.1).

The systematic accumulation of harmful aerosols in the air in populated areas is the cause of many diseases among their inhabitants. It leads to undesirable changes in the climate, forest, land, and all vital ecological systems [16, 17]. In the medical literature, a huge number of studies on the influence of concentrations of air pollutants on human health have been published. High, medium and even low levels of the main pollutants in the urban ambient air are the cause of numerous diseases and lead to serious and dangerous complications in chronically ill people, small children, the elderly, and pregnant women.

The authors of [18] focused on the risks of polluted air affecting respiratory diseases. Even low concentrations of air pollutants are dangerous for human health, and in particular for children, the elderly, and sick people

[19-21]. Other results in this direction are published in [22-24]. The damage from exposure to fine particles with aerodynamic diameters smaller than 2.5 microns ($PM_{2.5}$) is considered even greater, as it affects internal organs at the cellular level. Publications on this topic are [25-28]. Many other researchers also report on the combined effects of air pollution emissions, systematized in review papers [29-32]. A systematic overview of air pollution control policies and impacts is presented in [33].

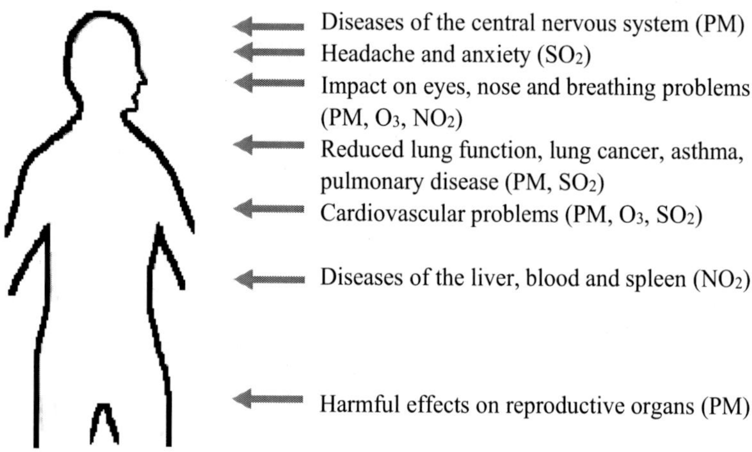

Figure 1.1. Impact of various air pollutants on human health.

1.3. Literature Review on Statistical Modeling in Environmental Science

To counteract the negative impact of air pollutants on nature and society, many researchers study and analyze the current state and causes of harmful emissions on a local, regional, and global scale. Analytical, analytical-numerical, statistical and, in recent years, ML data processing approaches developed by various researchers aim at building models for analysis, establishing classifications, prediction, and forecasting of time series. Variations and rapidly changing weather conditions are among the important factors in the formation and transport of pollution and are essential for the analysis of the time series of pollutants [34, 35].

In addition to meteorological and atmospheric variables, road transport time series and others are often used as predictors in the air pollutant modeling process. As predictors of secondary air pollutants (e.g., O_3), other relevant primary pollutants can be included. Furthermore, when these predictors influence with time delays, their lagged variables can also be included in the models. Less commonly, various "artificial" predictors such as hour, day of the week, dummy variables for outliers or some special cases can also be used as predictors in regression-type models.

Air pollution forecasting is a non-trivial task in which the atmospheric pollution concentrations at a given location and time are expected to be predicted based on existing data measurements of various factors. For research purposes, they are divided into global, regional, and local. From the point of view of the individual in the society, what is of practical value is the impact of local factors, more specifically, a given settlement, and taking into account the local climatic, geographical, industrial, and other types of characteristics and factors affecting the degree of pollution and the consequences related to human health [36].

1.3.1. Review of Mathematical and Statistical Studies on Air Pollution

Standard solutions for the outlined tasks produce computer numerical (mechanistic) models. They are used for simulating atmospheric chemical composition and atmospheric dispersion modeling systems based on mathematical and chemical equations describing pollutant transport and chemical diffusion processes [37-39]. A computational fluid dynamics model capable of simulating the dispersion of pollutants in a large urban environment is reported in [40]. In another recent paper [41], supercomputer-based numerical simulations using the finite volume method and semi-implicit difference schemes are employed for short-term prediction of extreme meteorological conditions and atmospheric air quality.

This class of approaches also includes research on numerical sensitivity analyses in air pollution, Monte-Carlo, and other mathematical approaches [42, 43]. These papers carry out a sensitive analysis of the model outputs from the large-scale Unified Danish Eulerian Model (UNI-DEM) - a typical deterministic numerical model, based on a partial differential problem, which involves 35 pollutants and 116 chemical reactions, of which 69 are time-dependent, and 47 are time-independent. In [42], efficient quasi-Monte Carlo algorithms using modified Sobol sequences, modified van der Corput sequences, a new lattice reflection rule, and multidimensional integration are developed for sensitivity analysis of a part of the output model results. In [43], this approach is further improved for a sensitivity study with respect to emission levels and some chemical reaction rates of the concentration variations of air pollutants, modeled by UNI-DEM.

However, the practical implementation of this type of numerical models presupposes the presence of detailed input numerical information on current air quality, monitored by local stations, remote sensing, forecasted weather conditions, data on the geographical terrain, and others. Also, one of the major properties of mechanistic models, as model-driven approaches, is the embedded causality, which is difficult to prove. These models are complex, and their creation usually requires significant computing resources. Given the complex nature of the processes forming the aerosols in the atmosphere, mechanical (deterministic) models cannot accurately predict the spatio-temporal variation of air pollutants [44] and they are not enough efficient for short- and medium-term forecasts. Therefore, these models are not sufficiently suitable for planning and regulation of air quality [45, 46].

A promising alternative to numerical modeling is a large group of statistical methods. From these ML allows the construction of effective predictive models that can be easily implemented even into mobile applications. As mentioned, two types of predictive regression approaches for forecasting time series can be systematized from the available literature: model-driven and data-driven. The model-driven approach mainly includes statistical and stochastic data modeling methods, parametric and nonparametric, and with additional conditions, a solution is found. In contrast, the characteristic of ML methods is that models learn from data, controlled by their hyperparameters. This is achieved through different ways of training the model by varying the sample data and obtaining a large number of models, from which the final model is selected according to given criteria.

Classical methods include multiple linear regression (MLR), nonlinear regressions, Principal Component Analysis (PCA), some numerical methods, stochastic Autoregressive Integrated Moving Average (ARIMA), seasonal ARIMA, gaseous air contamination modeling, and more. These methods provide models, describing simultaneously all data with a common preset and fixed dependence type. These statistical, -mathematical methods and hybrid approaches are used, for example, in [47-50]. The authors of [47] analyze and model tropospheric ozone in Warsaw, depending on its precursors for selected heat waves using PCA and MLR. Stochastic Box-Jenkins ARIMA and MLR models of PM_{10} are developed in [48, 49], and gaseous air pollution is studied in [50] for some Bulgarian cities.

A recent large-scale, extensive study using spatial interpolation and MLR found close air pollutant-meteorological interactions in China [51]. Another study also focused on the importance of meteorological conditions on air pollution [52]. In one study [53], univariate SARIMA models were built with intervention variables to reflect the outliers for $PM_{2.5}$ and PM_{10}. The MLR is implemented in [54] for PM_{10}, depending on temperature changes. The authors of [55] applied MLR, Loess seasonal and trend decomposition with ARIMA, and SARIMA models to analyze and compare the forecasts of PM_{10}. Other studies have incorporated the influence of atmospheric factors and pollutant modeling with MLR, ARIMA, and integrated ARFIMA [56, 57]. Paper [58] is devoted to build hybrid ARIMA-GARCH models of PM_{10} concentrations.

In [59] two-step SARIMA models are developed, where the weather variables are forecast at the first stage and PM_{10} – at the second stage. The models fit the observed data up to 86%. A similar approach is applied in [60]. Factor analysis with PCA and Promax rotation, and Box-Jenkins methodology is applied to examine univariate hourly time series of NO, NO_2, NOx, PM_{10}, SO_2 and O_3 in the town of Blagoevgrad, Bulgaria in [61]. Markov chains are adopted in [62] for modeling of PM_{10} air contamination. Other publications of this class, both for univariate and multivariate time series, including some for Bulgaria, are the following [63-66]. It should be noted that in the presence of the linear nature of the studied time series, some classical statistical methods such as ARIMA can provide adequate and sufficiently good predictions without yielding to complex advanced ML algorithms.

In addition to the study and modeling of different single pollutants, modeling the relationships between multiple pollutants is also an important task. In practice, there is a mutual influence between the components of the air, determined by chemical reactions, weather conditions, and the complex dynamics of emissions. There are several different types of methods in this field. For example, a vector type of multivariate ARIMA is implemented in [67], where 3- and 4 dimensional ARIMA models are built.

Another preferred method for studying mutual relationships between different factors is time-series Granger causality analysis [68]. It is applied in various fields. Among them is the study of the relations between air pollution and economic indicators [69], causal dynamics between CO_2 emissions, health expenditures and economic growth [70], causal effects of air pollution on health [71, 72], and others. In particular, although a small number of publications, have used Granger causality to study interdependencies between air pollutants' time series. In [73]. the authors develop a methodology for discovering causal links between the ozone variations, nitrogen oxides and local meteorological conditions, using Positive Matrix Factorization (PMF), k–means cluster analysis, and the Granger causality test. In [74] quantitative evidence is presented to verify the relative impacts of stationary emission sources on a number of air quality stations by applying time-series Granger causality. Classification models based on causality tests and different ML algorithms are reported in [75]. The author considered the causal- influence of the industrial pollutants NO_2, SO_2, CO and O_3 and meteorological variables on $PM_{2.5}$. Zhu et al. [76] proposed a spatio-temporal Granger causality approach which integrates different urban dynamic big data to select the most influential dataset for air quality estimation.

A recent comparison between ARIMA and ML results in the time series forecasting literature is presented in a review paper [77].

1.3.2. Review of Machine Learning Studies

In the last decade, the high-performance ML techniques for forecasting air pollution have dominated the literature. ML models are capable of extracting the hidden relationship between the input data and the target, as well as predicting with great accuracy empirical data of any kind. The corresponding algorithms exceed classical statistical methods in speed of execution and accuracy of forecasts, being able to reach 99% fitting with the data.

The most popular ML approaches are Artificial Neural Network (ANN), Multilayer Perception (MLP) and other variants of ANN, including Recurrent Neural Network (RNN) - a new time-related intelligent deep learning. Another large class of ML methods is based on decision trees, the most popular of which are Random Forests (RF), Classification and Regression Trees (CART), etc. High-performance models can also be obtained with Support Vector Machine (SVM), Genetic algorithm (GA), Multivariate Adaptive Regression Splines (MARS), and more, including the various developed hybrid approaches.

By the way, in the field of environmental science, engineering, medicine and other areas, the methods and publications with neural networks and the resulting new techniques – in particular, deep learning, LSTM, and related approaches [78] are significantly predominant. As for decision tree-based methods, the latter do not have such popularity in academic circles. At the same time, in almost all the world's major software competitions, decision-tree class methods unquestionably and categorically outperform ANN-based approaches. For example, in [79] it is discussed the dominance of the tree-based machine learning methods, reached the top ranks in the recent M5, Kaggle, Global Energy Forecasting (GEFCom), and other competitions, both in the accuracy and the uncertainty track, and achieving a higher performance level in comparison with deep-learning class methods. In this aspect, we hope that our monograph will make a further contribution to the challenges and promotion of these methods.

In [80], ANN models are constructed to predict PM_{10} pollution in Poland. ANN and PCA are combined to derive models of PM_{10} and $PM_{2.5}$ in [81]. Authors of [82] study PM_{10} concentrations designing six ML models, based on SVM regression, k-nearest neighbor regression (kNN), RF regression, gradient boosting regression (GBR), tweedie regression (TR), and Bayesian ridge regression (BRR). In [83], a common CART approach is proposed to address- the general nature of nonlinear dependence for PM_{10} concentrations. Assuming large samples of data, different aspects of CART models are explored, including the construction of additional predictors, building the stable CART models by stepwise predictor groups modeling and correcting model errors through a moving average (MA) process to achieve R^2=90% fit of the models to the original data. The complex relationships between air pollutants and meteorology are quantitatively revealed in [84] using Community Multiscale Air Quality (WRF-CMAQ), a traditional atmospheric model for more realistic simulation of chemical-meteorological processes, RF analysis and RNN. Accurate forecasts for 24-hours ahead of pollutants SO_2, NO_2, CO, $PM_{2.5}$, PM_{10}, and O_3 were obtained. In [85] monthly PM_{10} concentrations are forecasted using the previous values of PM_{10}, SO_2, NO, NO_2, CO and O_3 as input variables. The models are built using ARIMA, vector ARIMA (VARMA), MLP, SVM and MARS. Author of [86] studies the PM_{10} concentrations in Brunei-Muara district incorporating meteorological time series, MLR, RF, extreme gradient boosting (XgBoost) and ANN. PM level is approximated with up to $R^2 = 98\%$. Sophisticated models of time series of air pollutants are built using deep learning, including the long-short term memory (LSTM) approaches, which involve deep layers and massive neurons to achieve superior descriptive ability on the training set (see, for instance, [87, 88]. Authors of [89] applied RF, Bagged Classification and Regression Trees (Bagged CART), and Mixture Discriminant Analysis (MDA) for the hazard prediction of PM_{10} in 75 monitoring stations, in Barcelona, Spain. Hourly PM_{10} concentrations are forecasted in [90] using extreme gradient boosting. RNN models using MLP and Elman NN were built in [91] to forecast the daily maximum concentrations of SO_2, O_3, PM_{10}, NO_2, CO in the city of Palermo, Italy. To this class of results, we could recommend review papers [92-94].

Over the years, in the field of ML, growing attention is directed towards ensemble ML methods [95-97]. They are used for both classification and regression problems. These are characterized by the construction of numerous ensemble component models (learners) using the same algorithm and combining their resulting outcomes. A typical representative is RF consisting of a large number of unpruned CART trees. The most frequently used techniques include resampling, bagging, and boosting [95, 97]. When bagging, the trees in the ensemble are parallel and independent, and when boosting, they are sequential. The main advantage of the ensemble methods is that these lead to a dramatic decrease in test set errors and a significant reduction of variance [98].

Bagged trees and RF models for predicting fine particulate matter ($PM_{2.5}$) are built in [99]. An ensemble approach is applied in [100] to forecast $PM_{2.5}$ in the greater London area. Many models, including RF, bagging, and additive regression, were built and compared to single models with SVM, MLP, linear regression, and regression trees [101] to predict NO_2 concentration levels. It has been shown that ensemble models statistically outperform other models. Four ANN ensemble models and an innovative Fuzzy Inference Ensemble (FIE) model were proposed in [102] and are capable of estimating the concentration levels of O_3, CO, NO, NO_2, SO_2, PM_{10}, and $PM_{2.5}$. More ensemble methods, including the tree-based, are considered in [99-105].

Despite the good qualities of ANN or decision tree ensemble methods based on weak learners, random subspaces, and randomness in the algorithms, some of the created models can be unstable and lacking in predictive power [106, 107]. Selective ensemble algorithms are suggested to improve the generalization ability of the ensemble models. Overall, the goal is to identify and remove the weakest learners, which reduce the performance of the ensemble. This allows to build a new ensemble that is not only smaller in size, but also more accurate than ensembles generated by non-selective algorithms. Under development are different approaches for the construction of selective ensembles in the case of decision trees, for ANN or other types of learners that use multi-objective techniques, statistical measures, pruning techniques, and other [106-108]. More studies in the class of ML methods considered are [109-112]. Different approaches for improving regression models' accuracy, particularly residual correction using ARIMA, are presented in [113, 114, 83].

Recently, a special class of ML approaches applying the stacked generalization paradigm is gaining popularity. Stacked generalization (stacking) is a type of meta-modeling to combine the predictions of several heterogeneous ML models using another learning algorithm to learn and predict which combinations of models generally give better performance. The idea to combine the predictions of regression models of time series dates back to the 1970s in papers [115, 116]. In 1992, Wolpert [117] introduced the term stacking for classification problems, also adopted for regression by Breiman in [118].

In environmental science, stacking methods are still applied relatively rarely. For example, time series of air pollutants are modeled with weighted support vector regression (SVR), boosting and chance theory in [119], with selective techniques in [99], and more. In [120], a stacked ensemble model is developed for forecasting the daily average concentrations of $PM_{2.5}$ in Beijing, China, based on levels of other pollutants and meteorological data. The base models in the stacking strategy are built with LASSO, AdaBoost, XgBoost, and GA-MLP. Their predictions are stacked using SVM. It has been shown that the resulting stacked model outperforms all base models by achieving R2 = 90%. Similarly, to predict the levels of $PM_{2.5}$ Zhu et al. constructed an ensemble model based on decision trees, random forest (RF), Adaboost, GBDT, K-nearest neighbor (kNN), XgBoost, LightgBM, CatBoost, support vector regression (SVR), Stacking, Blending, and MLR, respectively [121]. The goodness of fit of all ensemble learning models reached about 0.92-0.94 or 92% to 94% fitting with the initial $PM_{2.5}$ data. An optimal combination with deep learning (stacked sparse autoencoder with a MLP) and ensemble learning is adopted to study hourly AQI index by exploring big data with meteorological conditions in [122].

The current state of ensemble methods, including stacking approaches, could be found in review papers [97, 105, 123, 124].

We will pay special attention to combined statistical analyses using methods with wavelet transform (WT) and the increasingly frequently applied discrete WT (DWT). DWT is used for the processing of signals, presented in numerical form, received from various measuring devices, sensor systems, medical devices and others. This type of empirical data contains noise, inaccuracies and outliers due to the measurement accuracy of the instrument used, external influences, and other reasons distorting the signal. To study time series, the classic Fourier analysis and the more powerful wavelet analysis are often applied, in the continuous and discrete case (see, for instance, the theoretical and applied aspects in [125, 126]). While Fourier analysis identifies the most important harmonics in time series, the wavelets decompose the signal both in frequencies and in time. The wavelet transform is frequently used in engineering and computer science for data compression, denoising, signal analysis, signal decomposition, and enhancing the model performance.

Recent publications in this field of environmental science are, for example, [127-130]. The authors of [127] enhanced the accuracy in PM_{10} forecast using the wavelet transform and an NN ensemble combining MLP, radial basis function, Elman NN, Support vector regression (SVR), and other base models to obtain a stacked model. A combination of function expansions in a wavelet series with ARIMA models is used in [128]. Correlation analysis and ANNs, including wavelet analysis to identify the linear and nonlinear mutual relations, respectively, between the air pollution index and meteorological variables in two Chinese cities, were applied in [129]. Twelve algorithms and a large number of meteorological predictors have been used to obtain coefficients of determination for the forecasts in the range of 88-89%. Air pollution data (SO_2, NO_2, PM_{10}, $PM_{2.5}$, O_3, and CO) and meteorological variables temperature, barometric pressure, humidity, and wind speed are modeled in [130] using wavelet denoising, detrended correlation analysis, and the long short-term memory (LSTM) approach.

In [131], the authors show that hybrid models coupled WT and ARIMA are more reliable in predicting future atmospheric PM pollution compared to the classical ARIMA method. Results from [132] demonstrate four different topologies of deep ANN for the prediction of $PM_{2.5}$ concentrations by using five levels of DWT. In addition, a hybrid NN composed of LSTM and 1D-CNN is built to improve the forecasts. Recently, an ensemble deep learning approach and wavelets were adopted in [133] to detect air pollution. Other results based on WT in environmental science can be found in [134-137].

However, one drawback of statistical models is that they do not consider the physics behind the data, and consequently, the developed model for a study area could not be applicable to other sites [138].

The combined modeling of air pollution data using a variety of ML methods provides an excellent means for design, analysis and revealing of interrelationships in complex relationships to obtain reliable and accurate forecasts. This type of results is of particular importance and contributes to solving the increasingly difficult issues related to reducing emissions harmful to the population and improving ambient air quality.

References

[1] Box, G. E., 1979. Robustness in the strategy of scientific model building. In *Robustness in statistics* (pp. 201-236). Academic Press.

[2] Akaike, H., 1974. A new look at the statistical model identification. *IEEE Transactions on Automatic Control*, 19(6), 716-723.

[3] Schwarz, G., 1978. Estimating the dimension of a model. *Annals of Statistics*, 6, pp. 461-464.

[4] Ding. J., Tarokh, V. and Yang, Y., 2018. Model selection techniques: An overview. *IEEE Signal Processing Magazine*, 35(6), pp. 16-34.

[5] Wolpert, D. H. and Macready, W. G., 1997. No free lunch theorems for optimization. *IEEE Transactions on Evolutionary Computation*, 1(1), pp. 67-82.

[6] IARC Working Group on the Evaluation of Carcinogenic Risks to Humans, 2016. Outdoor Air Pollution. *IARC Monographs on the Evaluation of Carcinogenic Risks to Humans*, 109. https://www.ncbi.nlm.nih.gov/books/NBK368024/pdf/Bookshelf_NBK368024.pdf.

[7] Directive 2008/50/EC of the European Parliament and of the Council of 21 May 2008 on ambient air quality and cleaner air for Europe, 2008. *Official Journal of the European Union*, L 152/1. https://eur-lex.europa.eu/eli/dir/2008/50/oj.

[8] EU Air Quality Standards, 2024. https://environment.ec.europa.eu/topics/air/air-quality/eu-air-quality-standards_en.

[9] Europe's Air Quality Status, 2024. https://www.eea.europa.eu//publications/europes-air-quality-status-2024.

[10] WHO Global Air Quality Guidelines: Particulate matter (PM2.5 and PM10), ozone, nitrogen dioxide, sulfur dioxide and carbon monoxide, 2021. https://iris.who.int/bitstream/handle/10665/345329/9789240034228-eng.pdf.

[11] EEA (European Environment Agency), 2024. *How Air Pollution Affects our Health.* https://www.eea.europa.eu/en/topics/in-depth/air-pollution 25 June 2024.

[12] European Air Quality Index (EAQI). https://airindex.eea.europa.eu/AQI/index.html.

[13] Executive Environment Agency (ExEA), Bulgaria. http://eea.government.bg/en.

[14] WHO, 2022. *Ambient (Outdoor) Air Pollution, Key Facts.* https://www.who.int/news-room/fact-sheets/detail/ambient-(outdoor)-air-quality-and-health

[15] EEA, 2023. *Health Impacts of Air Pollution.* https://www.eea.europa.eu/en/topics/in-depth/air-pollution/eow-it-affects-our-health

[16] Manisalidis, I., Stavropoulou, E., Stavropoulos, A. and Bezirtzoglou, E., 2020. Environmental and health impacts of air pollution: A review. *Frontiers of Public Health*, 8, 14.

[17] Gibson, J, 2015. Air pollution, climate change, and health. *The Lancet Oncology,* 16, e269.

[18] Bălă, G.-P., Râjnoveanu, R.-M., Tudorache, E., Motișan, R. and Oancea, C., 2021. Air pollution exposure—the (in)visible risk factor for respiratory diseases. *Environmental Science and Pollution Research*, 28(16), pp. 19615-19628.

[19] Finch, J., Riggs, D.W., O'Toole, T.E., Pope III C.A., Bhatnagar, A. and Conklin, D.J., 2019. Acute exposure to air pollution is associated with novel changes in blood levels of endothelin-1 and circulating angiogenic cells in young, healthy adults. *AIMS Environmental Science*, 6(4), pp. 265-276.

[20] Chen, Z., Wang, B., Hu, Y., Cui, X. and Shi, T., 2022. Short-term effects of low-level ambient air NO2 on the risk of incident stroke in Enshi city, China.

International Journal of Environmental Research and Public Health, 19(11), art. 6683.

[21] Ibrahim, M. F., Hod, R., Tajudin, M. A. B. A., Mahiyuddin, W. R. W., Nawi, A. M. and Sahani, M., 2022. Children's exposure to air pollution in a natural gas industrial area and their risk of hospital admission for respiratory diseases. *Environmental Research*, 210, art. 112966.

[22] Hamanaka, R. B. and Mutlu, G. M., 2018. Particulate matter air pollution: Effects on the cardiovascular system. *Frontiers in Endocrinology*, 9, art. 680.

[23] Zhu, L., Ge, X., Chen, Y., Zeng, X., Pan, W., Zhang, X., Ben, S., Yuan, Q., Xin, J., Shao, W. and Ge, Y., 2017. Short-term effects of ambient air pollution and childhood lower respiratory diseases. *Scientific reports*, 7(1), p. 4414.

[24] Wang, J., Lin, C., Chu, Y., Deng, H. and Shen, Z., 2023. Association between long-term exposure to air pollution and the risk of incident laryngeal cancer: a longitudinal UK Biobank-based study. *Environmental Science and Pollution Research*, 30(20), pp. 58295-58303.

[25] Kettunen, J., Lanki, T., Tiittanen, P., Aalto P. P., Koskentalo T., Kulmala M., Salomaa, V. and Pekkanen, J., 2007. Associations of fine and ultrafine particulate air pollution with stroke mortality in an area of low air pollution levels. *Stroke*, 38(3), pp. 918-922.

[26] He, F., Yanosky, J. D., Fernandez-Mendoza, J., Chinchilli, V. M., Al-Shaar, L., Vgontzas, A. N., Bixler, E. O. and Liao, D., 2022. Acute impact of fine particulate air pollution on cardiac arrhythmias in a population-based sample of adolescents: The Penn State child cohort. *Journal of the American Heart Association*, 11(18), e026370.

[27] Janssen, N. A., Fischer, H. P., Marra, M., Ameling, C. and Casse, F. R., 2013. Short-term effects of PM2.5, PM10 and PM2.5-10 on daily mortality in the Netherlands. *Science of the Total Environment*, 463-464, pp. 20-26.

[28] Kim, H., Kim, W. H., Kim, Y. Y. and Park, H. Y., 2020. Air pollution and central nervous system disease: a review of the impact of fine particulate matter on neurological disorders. *Frontiers in Public Health*, 8, p. 575330.

[29] Thangavel, P., Park, D. and Lee, Y. C., 2023. Recent insights into particulate matter (PM2.5)-mediated toxicity in humans: an overview. *International Journal of Environmental Research and Public Health*, 19(12), p. 7511.

[30] Dahlquist, M., Frykman, V., Hollenberg, J., Jonsson, M., Stafoggia, M., Wellenius, G. A. and Ljungman, P. L., 2023. Short-term ambient air pollution exposure and risk of out-of-hospital cardiac arrest in Sweden: A nationwide case-crossover study. *Journal of the American Heart Association*, 12(21), p. e030456.

[31] Shin, S., Burnett, R. T., Kwong, J. C., Hystad, P., van Donkelaar, A., Brook, J. R., Goldberg, M. S., Tu, K., Copes, R., Martin, R. V. and Liu, Y., 2019. Ambient air pollution and the risk of atrial fibrillation and stroke: a population-based cohort study. *Environmental Health Perspectives*, 127(8), p. 087009.

[32] Mohammadi, M. J., Fouladi Dehaghi, B., Mansourimoghadam, S., Sharhani, A., Amini, P. and Ghanbari, S., 2024. Cardiovascular disease, mortality and exposure to particulate matter (PM): a systematic review and meta-analysis. *Reviews on Environmental Health*, 39(1), pp. 141-149.

[33] Feng, T., Sun, Y., Shi, Y., Ma, J., Feng, C. and Chen, Z., 2024. Air pollution control policies and impacts: A review. *Renewable and Sustainable Energy Reviews*, 191, p. 114071.

[34] Seinfeld, J. and Pandis, S., 2016. *Atmospheric Chemistry and Physics: From Air Pollution to Climate Change, 3rd ed.* John Wiley & Sons, New Jersey, USA.

[35] Wilks D. S., 2011. *Statistical Methods in the Atmospheric Sciences*, 3nd ed. Elsevier, Amsterdam.

[36] Ravindra, K., Rattan, P., Mor, S. and Aggarwal, A., 2019. Generalized additive models: Building evidence of air pollution, climate change and human health. *Environment International*, 132, 104987.

[37] Brasseur, G. P. and Jacob, D. J., 2017. *Modeling of Atmospheric Chemistry.* Cambridge University Press, Cambridge, UK.

[38] Barratt, R., 2013. *Atmospheric Dispersion Modelling: An Introduction to Practical Applications.* Routledge, London, UK.

[39] Dimov, I., Georgiev, K., Ostromsky, T. and Zlatev, Z., 2004. Computational challenges in the numerical treatment of large air pollution models. *Ecological Modelling*, 179(2), pp. 187-203.

[40] Fernández-Pacheco, V. M., Álvarez-Álvarez, E., Blanco-Marigorta. E and Ackermann, T., 2023. CFD model to study PM10 dispersion in large-scale open spaces. *Scientific Reports*, 13(1), art. 5966.

[41] Starchenko, A. V., Danilkin, E. A., Prokhanov, S., Kizhner, L. and Shelmina, E., 2022. A supercomputer-based modeling system for short-term prediction of urban surface air quality. *Supercomputing Frontiers and Innovations*, 9(1), pp. 17-31.

[42] Todorov, V., Dimov, I., Ostromsky, T., Zlatev, Z., Georgieva, R. and Poryazov, S., 2021. Optimized quasi-Monte Carlo methods based on Van der Corput sequence for sensitivity analysis in air pollution modelling. In *Recent Advances in Computational Optimization: Results of the Workshop on Computational Optimization WCO 2020* (pp. 389-405). Springer International Publishing.

[43] Todorov, V. and Dimov, I., 2022. Innovative digital stochastic methods for multidimensional sensitivity analysis in air pollution modelling. *Mathematics*, 2022, 10, art. 2146.

[44] Alam, M. S. and McNabola, A., 2015. Exploring the modeling of spatiotemporal variations in ambient air pollution within the land use regression framework: Estimation of PM10 concentrations on a daily basis. *Journal of the Air & Waste Management Association*, 65(5), pp. 628-640.

[45] Goyal, P., Chan, A. T. and Jaiswal, N., 2006. Statistical models for the prediction of respirable suspended particulate matter in urban cities. *Atmospheric Environment*, 40, pp. 2068-2077.

[46] Jakeman, A. J., Simpson, R. W. and Taylor, J. A., 1988. Modeling distributions of air pollutant concentrations—III. The hybrid deterministic-statistical distribution approach. *Atmospheric Environment* (1967), 22(1), pp. 163-174.

[47] Rozbicka, K., Majewski, G., Rogula-Kozłowska, W. and Rozbicki, T., 2020. Tropospheric ozone assessment in urban environment–Warsaw case study of selected heat waves. *Journal of Atmospheric and Solar-Terrestrial Physics*, 209, p. 105418.

[48] Veleva, E., Filipova, M. and Zheleva, I., 2022, September. Statistical study of particulate matter (PM10) air contamination in the city of Vidin, Bulgaria. In *AIP Conference Proceedings* (Vol. 2522, No. 1). AIP Publishing.

[49] Minkova, I., Filipova, M. and Zheleva, I., 2023, November. Statistic study of particulate matter (PM10) air contamination in the city of Svishtov, Bulgaria. In *AIP Conference Proceedings* (Vol. 2953, No. 1). AIP Publishing.

[50] Nikolova, M., Filipova, M. and Zheleva, I., 2023, November. Statistic study of gaseous air contamination in the city of Ruse, Bulgaria. In *AIP Conference Proceedings* (Vol. 2953, No. 1). AIP Publishing.

[51] Liu, Y., Zhou, Y. and Lu, J., 2020. Exploring the relationship between air pollution and meteorological conditions in China under environmental governance. *Scientific Reports*, 10(1), p. 14518.

[52] Holst, J., Mayer, H. and Holst, T., 2008. Effect of meteorological exchange conditions on PM {sub 10} concentration. *Meteorologische Zeitschrift* (Berlin), 17, pp. 273-282.

[53] Veleva, E. and Zheleva, I., 2018. Statistical modeling of particle mater air pollutants in the city of Ruse, Bulgaria. In *MATEC Web of Conferences* (Vol. 145, p. 01010). EDP Sciences.

[54] Tsvetanova, I., Zheleva, I., Filipova, M. and Stefanova, A., 2018. Statistical analysis of ambient air PM10 contamination during winter periods for Ruse region, Bulgaria. In *MATEC Web of Conferences* (Vol. 145, p. 01007). EDP Sciences.

[55] Veleva, E. and Georgiev, I. R., 2020. Seasonality of the levels of particulate matter PM10 air pollutant in the city of Ruse, Bulgaria. In *AIP Conference Proceedings* (Vol. 2302, No. 1). AIP Publishing.

[56] Tsvetanova, I., Zheleva, I. T. and Filipova, M., 2019, October. Statistical study of the influence of the atmospheric characteristics upon the particulate matter (pm10) air pollutant in the city of Silistra, Bulgaria. In *AIP Conference Proceedings* (Vol. 2164, No. 1). AIP Publishing.

[57] Siew, L. Y., Chin, L. Y. and Wee, P. M. J., 2008. ARIMA and integrated ARFIMA models for forecasting air pollution index in Shah Alam, Selangor. Malaysian *Journal of Analytical Sciences*, 12(1), pp. 257-263.

[58] Veleva, E. and Zheleva, I., 2018, October. GARCH models for particulate matter PM10 air pollutant in the city of Ruse, Bulgaria. In *AIP Conference Proceedings* (Vol. 2025, No. 1). AIP Publishing.

[59] Gocheva-Ilieva, S., Ivanov, A. and Iliev, I., 2019, May. Exploring key air pollutants and forecasting particulate matter PM10 by a two-step SARIMA approach. In *AIP Conference Proceedings* (Vol. 2106, No. 1). AIP Publishing.

[60] Gocheva-Ilieva, S., Voynikova, D., Ivanov, A. and Stoimenova, M., 2019, October. Two-step time series analysis for air pollution in relation to weather conditions: Case study of Nessebar, Bulgaria. In *AIP Conference Proceedings* (Vol. 2164, No. 1). AIP Publishing.

[61] Gocheva-Ilieva, S. G., Ivanov, A. V., Voynikova, D. S. and Boyadzhiev, D. T., 2014. Time series analysis and forecasting for air pollution in small urban area: an SARIMA and factor analysis approach. *Stochastic Environmental Research and Risk Assessment*, 28(4), pp. 1045-1060.

[62] Veleva, E., Georgiev, I. R., Zheleva, I. and Filipova, M., 2020, December. Markov chains modelling of particulate matter (PM10) air contamination in the city of Ruse, Bulgaria. In *AIP Conference Proceedings* (Vol. 2302, No. 1). AIP Publishing.

[63] Tzanis, C. G., Alimissis, A., Philippopoulos, K. and Deligiorgi, D., 2019. Applying linear and nonlinear models for the estimation of particulate matter variability. *Environmental Pollution*, 246, pp. 89-98.

[64] Zheleva, I., Veleva, E. and Filipova, M., 2017, October. Analysis and modeling of daily air pollutants in the city of Ruse, Bulgaria. In *AIP Conference Proceedings* (Vol. 1895, No. 1). AIP Publishing.

[65] Veleva, E. and Zheleva, I., 2018. Statistical modeling of particle mater air pollutants in the city of Ruse, Bulgaria. In *MATEC Web of Conferences* (Vol. 145, p. 01010). EDP Sciences.

[66] Filipova, M., Zheleva, I. and Roussev, P., 2013. Characteristics of PM air pollution along Bulgaria - Romania Danube region, *Ecologica*, 71, pp. 215-217.

[67] Gocheva-Ilieva, S., Stoimenova, M., Ivanov, A., Voynikova, D. and Iliev, I., 2016, October. Stochastic univariate and multivariate time series analysis of PM2. 5 and PM10 air pollution: A comparative case study for Plovdiv and Asenovgrad, Bulgaria. In *AIP Conference Proceedings* (Vol. 1773, No. 1). AIP Publishing.

[68] Granger, C. W., 1969. Investigating causal relations by econometric models and cross-spectral methods. *Econometrica: Journal of the Econometric Society*, 37(3), pp. 424-438.

[69] Kumar, V. and Chander, R, 2016. Foreign direct investment and air pollution: Granger causality analysis. *IOSR Journal of Business and Management*, 2(20), pp. 12-17.

[70] Chaabouni, S., Zghidi, N. and Mbarek, M. B., 2016. On the causal dynamics between CO2 emissions, health expenditures and economic growth. *Sustainable Cities and Society*, 22, pp. 184-191.

[71] Bind, M. A., 2019. Causal modeling in environmental health. *Annual Review of Public Health*, 40(1), pp. 23-43.

[72] Schwartz, J., Bind, M. A. and Koutrakis, P., 2017. Estimating causal effects of local air pollution on daily deaths: effect of low levels. *Environmental Health Perspectives*, 125(1), pp. 23-29.

[73] Sfetsos, A. and Vlachogiannis, D., 2013. An analysis of ozone variation in the Greater Athens Area using Granger Causality. *Atmospheric Pollution Research*, 4(3), pp. 290-297.

[74] Chan, C. H., Juang, J. Y., Chu, T. H., Mao, C. H. and Huang, S. Y., 2023. A Novel Evaluation of Air Pollution Impact from Stationary Emission Sources to Ambient Air Quality via Time-Series Granger Causality. In *Earth Data Analytics for Planetary Health* (pp. 33-53). Singapore: Springer Nature Singapore.

[75] Wang, B., 2019. Applying machine-learning methods based on causality analysis to determine air quality in China. *Polish Journal of Environmental Studies*, 28(5), pp. 3877-3885.

[76] Zhu, J. Y., Sun, C. and Li, V. O., 2017. An extended spatio-temporal granger causality model for air quality estimation with heterogeneous urban big data. *IEEE Transactions on Big Data*, 3(3), pp. 307-319.

[77] Kontopoulou, V. I., Panagopoulos, A. D., Kakkos, I. and Matsopoulos, G. K., 2023. A review of ARIMA vs. machine learning approaches for time series forecasting in data rriven networks. *Future Internet*, 15, art. 255.

[78] Petropoulos, F., Apiletti, D., Assimakopoulos, V., Babai. M. Z., Barrow, D. K., Taieb, S. B. et al., 2022. Forecasting: theory and practice. *International Journal of Forecasting*, 38(3), pp. 705-871.

[79] Januschowski, T., Wang, Y., Torkkola, K., Erkkilä, T., Hasson, H. and Gasthaus, J., 2022. Forecasting with trees. *International Journal of Forecasting*, 38(4), pp. 1473-1481.

[80] Nidzgorska-Lencewicz, J., 2018. Application of artificial neural networks in the prediction of pm10 levels in the winter months: a case study in the tricity agglomeration, Poland. *Atmosphere*, 9(6), 203.

[81] Voukantsis, D., Karatzas, K., Kukkonen, J., Räsänen, T., Karppinen, A. and Kolehmainen, M., 2011. Intercomparison of air quality data using principal component analysis, and forecasting of PM10 and PM2.5 concentrations using artificial neural networks, in Thessaloniki and Helsinki. *Science of the Total Environment*, 409(7), pp. 1266-1276.

[82] Plocoste, T., and Laventure, S., 2023. Forecasting PM10 concentrations in the Caribbean area using machine learning models. *Atmosphere*, 14, art. 134.

[83] Gocheva-Ilieva, S., Voynikova, D., Stoimenova, M., Ivanov, A. and Iliev, I., 2019. Regression trees modeling of time series for air pollution analysis and forecasting. *Neural Computing and Applications*, 31(12), pp. 9023-9039.

[84] Feng, R., Zheng, H. J., Gao, H., Zhang, A. R., Huang, C., Zhang, J. X., Luo, K. And Fan, J. R., 2019. Recurrent Neural Network and random forest for analysis and accurate forecast of atmospheric pollutants: A case study in Hangzhou, China. *Journal of Cleaner Production*, 231, pp. 1005-1015.

[85] Lasheras, F., Nieto, P., Gonzalo, E., Bonavera, L. and de Cos Juez, F., 2020. Evolution and forecasting of PM10 concentration at the Port of Gijon (Spain). *Scientific Reports*, 10, art. 11716.

[86] Hong, W. Y., 2024. Meteorological variability and predictive forecasting of atmospheric particulate pollution. *Scientific Reports*, 14(1), art. 14.

[87] Xayasouk, T., Lee, H. M. and Lee, G., 2020. Air pollution prediction using long short-term memory (LSTM) and deep autoencoder (DAE) models. *Sustainability*, 12(6), art. 2570.

[88] Wang, J., Li, J., Wang, X., Wang, J. and Huang, M., 2021. Air quality prediction using CT-LSTM. *Neural Computing with Applications*, 33(10), pp. 4779-4792.

[89] Choubin, B., Abdolshahnejad, M., Moradi, E., Querol, X., Mosavi, A., Shamshirband, S. and Ghamisi, P., 2020. Spatial hazard assessment of the PM10 using machine learning models in Barcelona, Spain. *Science of the Total Environment*, 701, art. 134474.

[90] Wallek, S., Langner, M., Schubert, S., Franke, R. and Sauter, T., 2024. Hourly particulate matter (PM10) concentration forecast in Germany using extreme gradient boosting. *Atmosphere*, 15, p. 525.

[91] Brunelli, U., Piazza, V., Pignato, L., Sorbello, F. and Vitabile, S., 2007. Two-days ahead prediction of daily maximum concentrations of SO2, O3, PM10, NO2, CO in the urban area of Palermo, Italy. *Atmospheric Environment*, 41(14), pp. 2967-2995.

[92] Cabaneros, S. M., Calautit, J. K. and Hughes, B. R., 2019. A review of artificial neural network models for ambient air pollution prediction. *Environmental Modelling & Software*, 119, pp. 285-304.

[93] Zhang, B., Rong, Y., Yong, R., Qin, D., Li, M., Zou, G. and Pan, J., 2022. Deep learning for air pollutant concentration prediction: A review. *Atmospheric Environment*, 290, art. 119347.

[94] Tang, D., Zhan, Y. and Yang, F., 2024. A review of machine learning for modeling air quality: Overlooked but important issues. *Atmospheric Research*, art.107261.

[95] Opitz, D. and Maclin, R., 1999. Popular ensemble methods: An empirical study. *Journal of Artificial Intelligence Research*, 11, pp. 169-198.

[96] Sagi O. and Rokach L., 2018. Ensemble learning: A survey. *Wiley Interdisciplinary Reviews: Data Mining and Knowledge Discovery*, 8(4), e1249.

[97] Zhou, Z. H., 2012. *Ensemble Methods: Foundations and Algorithms*. CRC Press, Boca Raton.

[98] Breiman, L., 1998. Arcing classifiers. *The Annals of Statistics*, 26(3), pp. 801-849.

[99] Gu, K., Xia, Z. and Qiao, J., 2019. Stacked selective ensemble for PM 2.5 forecast. *IEEE Transactions on Instrumentation and Measurement*, 69(3), pp. 660-671.

[100] Yazdi, D., Kuang, Z., Dimakopoulou, K., Barratt, B., Suel, E., Amini, H., Lyapustin, A., Katsouyanni, K. and Schwartz, J., 2020. Predicting fine particulate matter (PM2.5) in the greater London area: An ensemble approach using machine learning methods. *Remote Sensing*, 12(6), 914.

[101] Masih, A., 2019. Application of ensemble learning techniques to model the atmospheric concentration of SO2. *Global Journal of Environmental Science and Management*, 5(3), pp. 309-318.

[102] Bougoudis, I., Iliadis, L. and Papaleonidas, A., 2014. Fuzzy inference ANN ensembles for air pollutants modeling in a major urban area: the case of Athens. In *Engineering Applications of Neural Networks: 15th International Conference,* EANN 2014, Sofia, Bulgaria, September 5-7, 2014. Proceedings 15 (pp. 1-14). Springer International Publishing.

[103] Aydogmus, H. Y., Ekinci, A. and Halil, I., 2015. Optimizing the monthly crude oil price forecasting accuracy via bagging ensemble models. *Journal of Economics and International Finance*, 7(5), p. 127.

[104] Mohammed, A. S., Asteris, P. G., Koopialipoor, M., Alexakis, D. E., Lemonis, M. E. and Armaghani, D. J., 2021. Stacking ensemble tree models to predict energy performance in residential buildings. *Sustainability*, 13, art. 8298.

[105] Mendes-Moreira, J., Soares, C., Jorge, A. M. and Sousa, J. F. D., 2012. Ensemble approaches for regression: A survey. *ACM Computing Surveys* (csur), 45(1), pp. 1-40.

[106] Zhou, Z. H., Wu, J. and Tang, W., 2002. Ensembling neural networks: many could be better than all. *Artificial intelligence*, 137(1-2), pp. 239-263.

[107] Zhou, Z. H. and Tang, W., 2003. Selective ensemble of decision trees. In *Rough Sets, Fuzzy Sets, Data Mining, and Granular Computing: 9th International*

Conference, RSFDGrC 2003, Chongqing, China, May 26–29, 2003 Proceedings 9 (pp. 476-483). Springer Berlin Heidelberg.

[108] Zhu, X., Ni, Z., Cheng, M., Jin, F., Li, J. and Weckman, G., 2018. Selective ensemble based on extreme learning machine and improved discrete artificial fish swarm algorithm for haze forecast. *Applied Intelligence*, 48, pp. 1757-1775.

[109] Wang, P., Liu, Y., Qin, Z. and Zhang, G., 2015. A novel hybrid forecasting model for PM10 and SO2 daily concentrations. *Science of the Total Environment*, 505, pp. 1202-1212.

[110] Sayegh, A. S., Munir, S. and Habeebullah, T. M., 2014. Comparing the performance of statistical models for predicting PM10 concentrations. *Aerosol and Air Quality Research*, 14(3), pp. 653-665.

[111] Sethi, J. K. and Mittal, M., 2019. A new feature selection method based on machine learning technique for air quality dataset. *Journal of Statistics and Management Systems*, 22(4), pp. 697-705.

[112] Xu, Y., Liu, H. and Duan, Z., 2020. A novel hybrid model for multi-step daily AQI forecasting driven by air pollution big data. *Air Quality, Atmosphere & Health*, 13, pp. 197-207.

[113] Pankratz, A., 1991. *Forecasting with Dynamic Regression Models*. John Wiley & Sons, New York.

[114] Firmino, P. R. A., de Mattos Neto, P. S. and Ferreira, T. A., 2015. Error modeling approach to improve time series forecasters. *Neurocomputing*, 153, pp. 242-254.

[115] Bates, J. M. and Granger, C. W., 1969. The combination of forecasts. *Journal of the Operational Research Society*, 20(4), pp. 451-468.

[116] Newbold, P. and Granger, C. W., 1974. Experience with forecasting univariate time series and the combination of forecasts. *Journal of the Royal Statistical Society: Series A (General),* 137(2), pp. 131-146.

[117] Wolpert, D., 1992. Stacked generalization. *Neural Networks*, 5, pp. 241-259.

[118] Breiman, L., 1996. Stacked regressions. *Machine Learning*, 24, pp. 49-64.

[119] Eldakhly, N. M., Aboul-Ela, M. and Abdalla, A., 2018. A novel approach of weighted support vector machine with applied chance theory for forecasting air pollution phenomenon in Egypt. *International Journal of Computational Intelligence and Applications*, 17(01), p. 1850001.

[120] Zhai, B. and Chen, J., 2018. Development of a stacked ensemble model for forecasting and analyzing daily average PM2.5 concentrations in Beijing, China. *Science of the Total Environment*, 635, pp. 644-658.

[121] Zhu, Y., Liu, C. and Ma, J., 2022, December. Prediction of PM2. S concentration in Changchun based on ensemble learning model. In *2022 18th International Conference on Computational Intelligence and Security* (CIS) (pp. 79-83). IEEE.

[122] Wang, Z., Chen, H., Zhu, J. and Ding, Z., 2021. Multi-scale deep learning and optimal combination ensemble approach for AQI forecasting using big data with meteorological conditions. *Journal of Intelligent and Fuzzy Systems*, 40(3), pp. 5483-5500.

[123] Rybarczyk, Y. and Zalakeviciute, R., 2018. Machine learning approaches for outdoor air quality modelling: A systematic review. *Applied Sciences*, 8(12), p. 2570.

[124] Masih, A., 2019. Machine learning algorithms in air quality modeling. *Global Journal of Environmental Science and Management*, 5(4), pp. 515-534.

[125] Pinsky, M. A., 2023. *Introduction to Fourier Analysis and Wavelets* (Vol. 102). American Mathematical Society.

[126] Broughton, S. A. and Bryan, K., 2018. *Discrete Fourier Analysis and Wavelets: Applications to Signal and Image Processing,* 2nd ed. John Wiley & Sons.

[127] Siwek, K. and Osowski, S., 2012. Improving the accuracy of prediction of PM10 pollution by the wavelet transformation and an ensemble of neural predictors. *Engineering Applications of Artificial Intelligence*, 25(6), pp. 1246-1258.

[128] Mandrikova, O., Fetisova, N. and Polozov, Y., 2021. Hybrid model for time series of complex structure with ARIMA components. *Mathematics*, 9, art. 1122.

[129] Guo, Q., He, Z., Li, S., Li, X., Meng, J., Hou, Z., Liu, J. and Chen, Y., 2020. Air pollution forecasting using artificial and wavelet neural networks with meteorological conditions. *Aerosol and Air Quality Research*, 20(6), pp. 1429-1439.

[130] Zhang, Z., Chen, H. and Huang, X., 2023. Prediction of air quality combining wavelet transform, DCCA correlation analysis and LSTM model. *Applied Sciences*, 13(5), art. 2796.

[131] Aladağ, E., 2021. Forecasting of particulate matter with a hybrid ARIMA model based on wavelet transformation and seasonal adjustment. *Urban Climate*, 39, 100930.

[132] Galvão, S. L. J., Matos, J. C. O., Kitagawa, Y. K. L., Conterato, F. S., Moreira, D. M., Kumar, P. and Nascimento, E. G., S., 2022. Particulate matter forecasting using different deep neural network topologies and wavelets for feature augmentation. *Atmosphere*, 13(9), atr. 1451.

[133] Abbas, Z. and Raina, P., 2024. A wavelet enhanced approach with ensemble based deep learning approach to detect air pollution. *Multimedia Tools and Applications*, 83(6), pp. 17531-17555.

[134] Bai, Y., Li, Y., Wang, X., Xie, J. and Li, C., 2016. Air pollutants concentrations forecasting using back propagation neural network based on wavelet decomposition with meteorological conditions. *Atmospheric Pollution Research*, 7(3), pp. 557-566.

[135] Ebrahimi-Khusfi, Z., Taghizadeh-Mehrjardi, R., Kazemi, M. and Nafarzadegan, A. R., 2021. Predicting the ground-level pollutants concentrations and identifying the influencing factors using machine learning, wavelet transformation, and remote sensing techniques. *Atmospheric Pollution Research*, 12(5), 101064.

[136] Liu, B., Yu, X., Chen, J. and Wang, Q., 2021. Air pollution concentration forecasting based on wavelet transform and combined weighting forecasting model. *Atmospheric Pollution Research*, 12(8), 101144.

[137] Taşağıl Arslan, G. N. and Kılıç Depren, S., 2024. Optimizing air quality predictions: A discrete wavelet transform and long short-term memory approach with wavelet-type selection for hourly PM10 concentrations. *Journal of Chemometrics*, 38(4), p. e3539.

[138] Shahraiyni, T. H. and Sodouli, S., 2016. Statistical modeling approaches for PM10 prediction in urban areas: a review of 21st-century studies. *Atmosphere*, 7(2), art. 15.

Chapter 2

Time Series and Data Pre-Processing

Abstract

This chapter introduces basic concepts and notations for time series analysis and modeling. The basic steps for initial data processing are explained. Some recommendations and critiques of popular pre-processing tools are presented.

Keywords: air pollutant, autoregressive process, bias, coefficient of determination, ensemble model, forecasting, index of agreement, lagged variable, machine learning (ML), stationarity, time series

2.1. The Basic Concepts of Time Series

We will consider the modeling using regression type methods. The purpose of the regression model is both to describe and predict the observed data, and to make it possible to obtain forecasts for the future moments in time. There is a large volume of literary sources in which the classic theoretical and applied aspects of such models are developed [1, 2].

In the physical sense, time t is a continuous value, and accordingly, depending on it, the real variables of air pollutants, meteorological, atmospheric and other quantities are continuous functions of t. When measuring specific values in the discrete case of each real quantity, a set of data is accumulated that makes up the time series. A time series $\{Y_t\}$ is a sequence of data arranged according to time. The general form is

$$Y = \{Y_t\}_{t=1}^{N} = \{Y_1, Y_2, \dots, Y_t, \dots, Y_N\}, \quad Y_t \in \mathbb{R} \tag{2.1}$$

where the time t takes values 1, 2, 3, ..., *N*, *N* is the number of observations (sample size),$\mathbb{R}$ is the set of real numbers. For simplicity, we will assume that the data are equidistant, on a fixed scale (daily average, monthly average, annual average, etc.). When the series (2.1) is examined independently, it is called univariate time series. Modeling in this case is sought as a dependence between each observation Y_t and several of its previous ones $Y_{t-1}, Y_{t-2}, ...$ Time series, constructed with a fixed time indentation back is usually called a lagged variable. A modeling process accounting for lagged variables is called autoregressive.

When we consider Y from (2.1) in dependence on other accompanying time series as well, we have a multivariate time series problem. In addition to numerical time series of the type (2.1), we will also use data time series with categorical and string values. Examples of such type of variables are wind direction, weather conditions, date-time variables, car traffic conditions, and others that accept one of a finite number of string values for each given t. For example, wind direction can be coded S (Sud), NNE (Northeast), etc.

In the multidimensional case, we will consider that r independent variables (or predictors) of numerical or categorical type $X_{1,t}, X_{2,t}, .., X_{r,t}$ are set, each of them represented as a vector relative to t

$$\mathbf{X} = \{X_t\} = \left(X_{1,t}, X_{2,t}, .., X_{r,t}\right), \ \ t = 1,2,\ldots,N, \tag{2.2}$$

where $\mathbf{X}$ denotes their common matrix.

In our considerations, the main goal will be to build models that establish an explicit type of dependence of Yon the predictors, allowing possible prediction at future times.

Let the time series Y of the pollutant be the dependent variable. The explicit form of the dependence of Y (model) on X is sought in the form:

$$\{Y_t\} = \{f(X_t)\} + \{\varepsilon_t\}, \tag{2.3}$$

where $\{\varepsilon_t\}$ is the time series of errors (residuals). The model is

$$\{\hat{Y}_t\} = \{f(X_t)\}, \tag{2.4}$$

or simply written $\hat{Y} = f(\mathbf{X})$, where f is a non-linear real-valued function.

Often, the current value of the time series depends on one or more of its previous values for each t. In these cases, lagged variables have to be introduced. The lagged variable with k lags ($k = 1,2,\ldots$) is calculated by the formula

$$\{Y_t < k >\} = Y_{t-k}, \ \ t = k+1, k+2, ... \tag{2.5}$$

The k initial values in (2.5) can be set equal to Y_1, the time series mean, or other value, and the latter can be included or not in the models as needed.

In the most general case using lagged variables of all variables (2.2) in the analyses, this dependence is written as described in [3]

$$Y_t = f\big(Y_{t-1},..,Y_{t-p'},X_{1,t},...,X_{r,t},\\ X_{1,t-1},...,X_{1,t-q_1'},...,X_{r,t-1},...,X_{r,t-q_r'}\big) + \varepsilon_t, \tag{2.6}$$

where f is a non-linear real-valued function dependent on the values of the dependent variable in several previous moments $t-1,...,t-p'$, predictors X in the previous and/or current time moments and ε_t is the model error or residual. The residual time series is calculated from the expression

$$\varepsilon = Y - f(\mathbf{X}), \tag{2.7}$$

and is assumed to be uncorrelated with zero mean and constant variance σ^2 (white noise), i.e., $\varepsilon \in N(0, \sigma^2)$.

Another basic concept of time series is the concept of stationarity. A series is stationary when its probability distribution, mean and variance do not change over time. By the way, the prevailing in practice time series data are nonstationary and have at least one trend. In addition, data presented in time series can have highly variable behavior with seasonal and cyclical changes, sharp spikes and falls, and other features. Given this specificity, their modeling is not a trivial task.

2.2. Data Pre-Processing

As a modeling rule, we have raw data obtained automatically, collected from different sources, etc. They often have missing values, errors, duplication, mixed data type, different measurement units, and others. The process of statistical modeling begins with their careful initial pre-processing, which can take quite some time. One of the first procedures is to determine the type of the variables - scale, categorical, etc., check to remove unnecessary spaces, wrong symbols, convert to the correct units of measurement, remove apparently inappropriate values and variables, and more. Basic tools for this type of initial processing are descriptive statistics, graphing and analysis of numerical data graphics, distribution study, probability-probability (P-P) plots, quartile-quartile (Q-Q) plots and more.

When there are missing values in the initial data, substitution is done using different approaches. The most commonly applied are linear interpolation, substitution with the sample mean, use of ML method to predict and fill in missing values, and others. A practical guide for handling missing data and accompanied by examples is provided in [4].

Also, sometimes aggregating the data gives a more accurate idea of its nature and features important to the purpose of the study.

To improve the distribution and stabilize the variance, an initial transformation of the variables is often recommended. For time series, such transformations are, for example, logarithmic, Box-Cox, Yeo-Johnson, etc. [2, 5]. When there are negative values, we "lift" the entire sample using shift parameter - a suitably chosen constant C to calculate a natural logarithm, for example with a formula of the form

$$y_t^{\mathrm{Ln}} = \ln(x_t + C). \tag{2.8}$$

A basic transformation from the class of so-called power transformations is that of Box-Cox [6]. When $x_t > 0$, it is set with the expression

$$y_t^{\mathrm{BC}}(x_t, \lambda) = \begin{cases} \frac{x_t^{\lambda}-1}{\lambda}, & \lambda \neq 0 \\ \ln(x_t), & \lambda = 0 \end{cases}. \tag{2.9}$$

The parameter λ in (2.9) is usually estimated by the likelihood function. However, some critical notes, recent new improvements and appropriate goodness-of-fit tests for determining λ could be found in [7].

The power transformation of Yeo-Johnson is a generalization of (2.9) [8]. It is set with the expression

$$y_t^{\mathrm{YJ}}(x_t, \lambda) = \begin{cases} \frac{(x_t+1)^{\lambda}-1}{\lambda}, & x_t \geq 0, \lambda \neq 0 \\ \ln(x_t + 1), & x_t \geq 0, \lambda = 0 \\ -\frac{(1-x_t)^{2-\lambda}-1}{2-\lambda}, & x_t < 0, \lambda \neq 2 \\ \text{-}\ln(1 - x_t), & x_t < 0, \lambda = 2 \end{cases}, \quad \lambda \in [-2,2]. \tag{2.10}$$

In (2.10) λ could be found using the likelihood function or simply by sampling at different points in the interval [-2,2] and checking for normality of each of these transformed samples by the specified goodness of fit statistical tests. If the data contain many high extreme values (outliers), they can be transformed using the inverse hyperbolic sine (IHS) transformation, regardless of the sign of the argument [9, 10]:

$$y_t^{\mathrm{IHS}} = \frac{sinh^{-1}(\lambda x_t)}{\lambda} = \ln\left(\frac{\lambda x_t + \sqrt{(\lambda x_t)^2 + 1}}{\lambda}\right). \tag{2.11}$$

Most often, the parameter λ in (2.11) is set equal to 1. The IHS transformation is also appropriate to handle right-skewed distributions. The re-transformation is done with the $sinh(\lambda y)$ function.

The effect of transforming with (2.11) is illustrated in Figure 2.1. Figure 2.1(a) shows box-plots of three variables before transformation, and Figure 2.1(b) - after their transformation according to (2.11) for $\lambda = 1$.

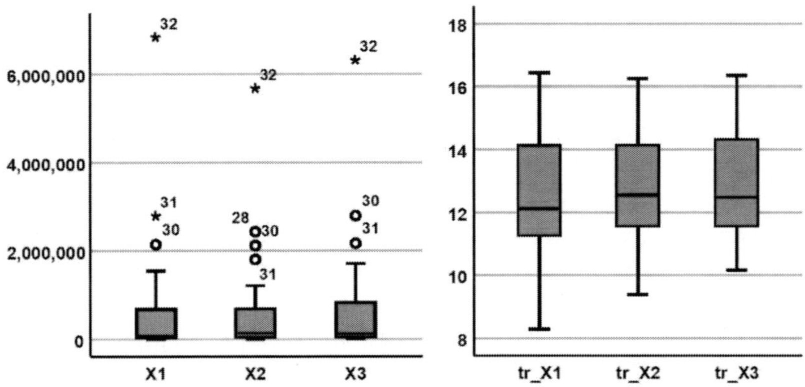

(a) (b)

Figure 2.1. Example of distribution enhancement: (a) box-plot of the initial variable; (b) box-plot after transformation using (2.11).

A sequence combining several transformations is also possible.

Another common problem in time series data is the presence of strong multicollinearity between variables, especially between variables considered independent in linear regression models. The term "multicollinearity" was introduced by Ragnar Frisch back in 1934 [11]. Multicollinearity means that between two or more variables, there is a linear type of dependence and large correlation coefficients in absolute value. In cases of multiple linear regression (MLR) models, this can deteriorate the accuracy and adequacy of the created models and lead to the calculation of biased estimates of the model coefficients. Fortunately, this problem does not significantly affect ML methods and nonlinear type dependency modeling.

Various inefficient methods for identifying and removing multicollinear variables exist in the literature. However, there is no practical justification for removing correlated variables from regression analysis, and doing so may constitute scientific misconduct [12]. Including collinear data does not reduce the predictive power or reliability of the model as a whole [13], and does not reduce the accuracy of coefficient estimates [14]. It should be borne in mind that when applying a stepwise regression, Variational Inflation Index (VIF), formal removal of correlated variables does not guarantee solving the problem and does not even lead to an improvement in the accuracy and adequacy of the models [15].

One way to detect and reduce unwanted multicollinearity is to calculate the overall correlation matrix of all variables, for example with Principal Component Analysis (PCA). When the determinant of this matrix is close to zero, it means that we have highly correlated (almost parallel) columns in the database. This collinearity can be naturally large, such as the close relations in air pollution data, financial data, etc. In this case, the correlated variables are first identified and assessed as to whether one is a close consequence of the other (for example, the relationship between a company's turnover and profits), in which case one variable can be removed.

To overcome collinearity, PCA and factor analysis with factor rotation could also be used to transform the variables into uncorrelated or less correlated latent factor variables. If the problem persists, it should be performed a factor analysis with grouping of the correlated variables into new, fewer factors (see also [16]).

Problems with correlated data can also be resolved by transforming them to a chosen type of distribution and checking for collinearity with the outcome variables.

2.3. Model-Performance Measures and Model Evaluation

When choosing a model, various statistics are used to evaluate its performance, adequacy, quality of the model's prediction to the original data and its ability to predict new data.

The most widely used statistical indicators for time series are: the coefficient of determination R^2 and the measures of errors such as the mean square error (MSE), root mean square error (RMSE), mean absolute error

(MAE) and the mean absolute percentage error (MAPE). These statistics are calculated by the expressions:

$$R^2 = \frac{\left\{\sum_{t=1}^{N}(P_t-\bar{P})(Y_t-\bar{Y})\right\}^2}{\sum_{t=1}^{N}(P_t-\bar{P})^2 . \sum_{t=1}^{N}(Y_t-\bar{Y})^2}, \tag{2.12}$$

$$MSE = \frac{1}{N}\sum_{t=1}^{N}(Y_t - P_t)^2, \quad RMSE = \sqrt{\frac{1}{N}\sum_{t=1}^{N}(Y_t - P_t)^2}, \tag{2.13}$$

$$MAE = \frac{1}{N}\sum_{t=1}^{N}|Y_t - P_t|, \quad MAPE = \frac{100}{N}\sum_{t=1}^{N}\left|\frac{Y_t-P_t}{Y_t}\right|, \tag{2.14}$$

where P_t is the model-predicted value of Y_t at time t, $\bar{Y}$ and $\bar{P}$ denote the mean values of the target and its predictions, respectively, N is the size of the modeled sample. A better model is considered one that has an R^2 close to 1 and small errors. Moreover, the MSE and RMSE depend on the units of measurement, which should be taken into account when comparing the accuracy of the different models. It should also be borne in mind that RMSE varies with the variability within the distribution of error magnitudes and with errors, as well as with the average-error magnitude (MAE) [17]. In the case of MAPE, apparently this measure can become unusable at Y_t close to zero, due to the instability of the relative computational error.

An alternative to the coefficient of determination is the Willmott index of agreement (IA), determined in [18] by the expression

$$IA = d = 1 - \frac{\sum_{t=1}^{N}(Y_t-P_t)^2}{\sum_{t=1}^{N}(|P_t-\bar{Y}|+|Y_t-\bar{Y}|)^2}. \tag{2.15}$$

The IA is not a measure of correlation or association in the formal sense but rather a measure of the degree to which a model's predictions are error-free [18].

In addition to the above measures, we should also mention some measures used to assess the bias of the model from the original data. For this purpose, mean bias error (MBE) and mean fractional bias (MFB) are most commonly used

$$MBE = \frac{1}{N}\sum_{t=1}^{N}(Y_t - P_t) = \bar{Y} - \bar{P}, \quad MFB = \frac{2}{N}\sum_{t=1}^{N}\frac{Y_t-P_t}{Y_t+P_t}. \tag{2.16}$$

The following relation is valid:

$$MBE \leq MAE \leq RMSE. \tag{2.17}$$

Other measures to evaluate the performance of predictive models can be found in [19-23].

One of the standard assumptions for a regression-type model is that the error terms (or residuals) ε_i and ε_j associated with the ith and jth observations are not correlated with each other. The presence of a correlation in errors means that there is information left in the data that is not captured by the evaluated model. It follows that in order to obtain an adequate model, it is necessary to carry out diagnostics of the residuals. This could be achieved by analyzing their ACF, whose coefficients should not leave the confidence interval. In addition, various statistical tests can be used, such as the Durbin-Watson, Ljung-Box portfolio, Box-Pierce, Breusch–Godfrey test, Kolmogorov-Smirnov test or Shapiro-Wilk test to check the normality of residuals [24].

In addition to the specified criteria, after building a model, its predictive quality is also evaluated for the cases from the test sample that did not participate in building the model itself. A model is chosen that shows a good prognostic quality. In ML, the verification of predictive accuracy is also carried out with various methods such as cross-validation, variation of holdout sample percentages, and others.

When more models show close statistics with the best values according to the selected criteria, the principle of parsimony could be applied [1, 25].

References

[1] Box, G. E. P., Jenkins, G. M., Reinsel, G. S., Ljung, G. M., 2016. *Time Series Analysis, Forecasting and Control*, 5th edn., John Wiley & Sons. Inc, New Jersey.

[2] Mills, T. C., 2019. *Applied Time Series Analysis: A Practical Guide to Modeling and Forecasting.* Academic press.

[3] Gocheva-Ilieva, S., Voynikova, D., Stoimenova, M., Ivanov, A. and Iliev, I., 2019. Regression trees modeling of time series for air pollution analysis and forecasting. *Neural Computing and Applications*, 31(12), pp. 9023-9039.

[4] Van Buuren, S., 2018. *Flexible Imputation of Missing Data.* CRC Press.

[5] Izenman J., 2008. *Modern Multivariate Statistical Techniques. Regression, Classification, and Manifold Learning*. Springer, New York.

[6] Box, G. E. P. and Cox, D. R., 1964. An analysis of transformations. *Journal of the Royal Statistical Society*, 26(2), pp. 211-252.

[7] Asar, O., Ilk, O. and Dag, O., 2017. Estimating Box-Cox power transformation parameter via goodness-of-fit tests. *Communications in Statistics - Simulation and Computation*, 46(1), pp. 91-105.

[8] Yeo, I. K. and Johnson, R. A., 2000. A new family of power transformations to improve normality or symmetry. *Biometrika*, 87(4), pp. 954-959.

[9] Burbidge, J. B., Magee, L. and Robb, A. L., 1988. Alternative transformations to handle extreme values of the dependent variable. *Journal of the American Statistical Association*, 83(401), pp. 123-127.

[10] Aihounton, G. B. and Henningsen, A., 2021. Units of measurement and the inverse hyperbolic sine transformation. *The Econometrics Journal*, 24(2), pp. 334-35.

[11] Frisch, R., 1934. *Statistical confluence analysis by means of complete regression systems*, Institute of Economics, Oslo University, publ. no. 5.

[12] Wikipedia, 2024. *Multicollinearity*, https://en.wikipedia.org/wiki/Multicollinearity.

[13] Goldberger, A. S., 1991. *A Course in Econometrics* (Ch. 23), Harvard University Press, Cambridge.

[14] Gujarati, D. N., 2004. *Basic Econometrics* (Ch. 10), 4th ed., McGraw−Hill.

[15] Kalnins, A. and Praitis Hill, K., 2023. The VIF score. What is it good for? Absolutely nothing. *Organizational Research Methods*, https://journals.sagepub.com/doi/10.1177/10944281231216381.

[16] Lafi, S. Q. and Kaneene, J. B., 1992. An explanation of the use of principal-components analysis to detect and correct for multicollinearity. *Preventive Veterinary Medicine*, 13(4), pp. 261-275.

[17] Willmott, C. J. and Matsuura, K., 2005. Advantages of the mean absolute error (MAE) over the root mean square error (RMSE) in assessing average model performance. *Climate research*, 30(1), pp. 79-82.

[18] Willmott, C., 1981. On the validation of models. *Phys. Geogr*. 2(2), pp. 184-194. https://doi.org/10.1080/02723646.1981.10642213

[19] Estrada, M., Camarillo, M. E. G., Parraguirre, M. E. S., Edgar, M., Castillo, G., Juárez, E. and Gómez, M. J., 2020. Evaluation of several error measures applied to the sales forecast system of chemicals supply enterprises. *International Journal of Business Administration*, 11, 39.

[20] Gerds, T. A., Cai, T. and Schumacher, M. 2008. The performance of risk prediction models, *Biometrical Journal: Journal of Mathematical Methods in Biosciences*, 50 (4), pp. 457-479.

[21] Hyndman, R. J. and Koehler, A. B. 2006. Another look at measures of forecast accuracy. *International journal of forecasting*, 22 (4), pp. 679-688.

[22] Wallström, P., 2009. *Evaluation of forecasting techniques and forecast errors, with focus on intermittent demand.* Doctoral dissertation, Lulea: Lulea University of Technology.

[23] Frías-Paredes, L., Mallor, F., Gastón-Romeo, M. and León, T., 2018. Dynamic mean absolute error as new measure for assessing forecasting errors. *Energy conversion and management*, 162, 176-188.

[24] Mienye, I. D. and Sun, Y., 2022. A survey of ensemble learning: Concepts, algorithms, applications, and prospects. *IEEE Access*. 16(10), pp. 99129-99149.

[25] Forster, M. R., 2000. Key concepts in model selection: Performance and generalizability. *Journal of mathematical psychology*, 44(1), pp. 205-231.

Chapter 3

Stochastic and Machine Learning Modeling Methods

Abstract

This chapter presents the conceptual foundations of the main modeling methods used throughout the book. A description of a total of 10 methods for machine learning is given, divided into four groups: stochastic and mathematical, basic machine learning methods, ensemble learning, and hybrid methods. The mathematical basis of the methods is also presented. The pros and cons of the methods are indicated. In addition, some useful recommendations for their application are given, gained from the personal experience of the authors of the current book. Emphasis is also placed on the more important aspects of the application of the methods for the case of time series. Some examples are also given.

Keywords: autoregression, bagging, boosting, cross-validation, decision trees, ensemble, forecasting, machine learning, prediction, stacking, supervised method

3.1. An Outline of the Modeling Methods Used

The empirical case studies presented in this book are based on a variety of approaches. They can be classified into four main groups: classic stochastic and mathematical methods, basic machine learning (ML) methods, ensemble tree-based ML, and hybrid ones.

Figure 3.1 shows an outline of this classification.

3.2. Stochastic and Mathematical Modeling of Time Series

The first group of methods in the scheme shown in Figure 3.1 includes some classic time series methods. The following chapters apply a number of such methods, including ARIMA, Discrete Wavelet Transform (DWT), Temporal Causal Modeling (TCM), Principal Component Analysis (PCA), Factor analysis (FA), Multiple Linear Regression (MLR) and more. We will briefly describe the first three of them.

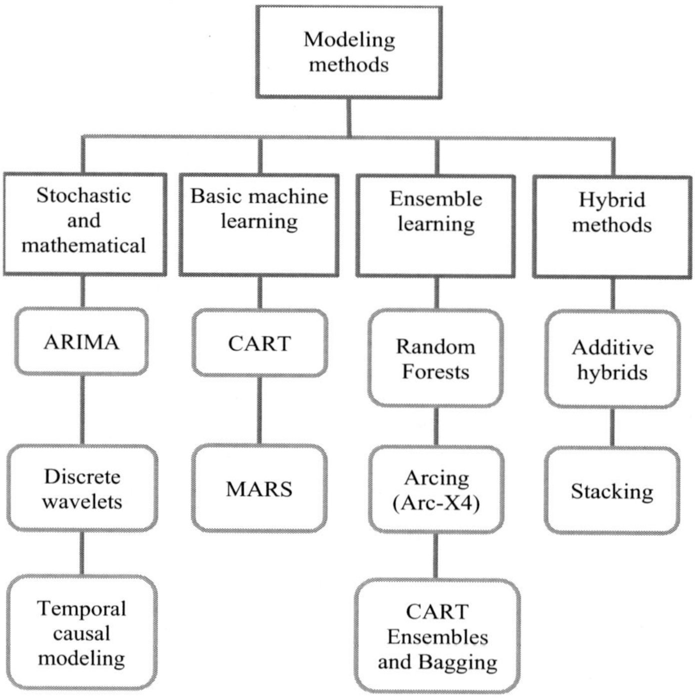

Figure 3.1. Outline of the modeling methods used in the book.

3.2.1. ARIMA Method

The Autoregressive Integrated Moving Average (ARIMA) method is a popular class of stochastic parametric methods for forecasting and time series analysis. The algorithm and its computational foundations were developed by Box and Jenkins in 1970 [1]. The approach is also known as the Box-Jenkins methodology. It can be used to model univariate and multivariate time series, seasonal type series, vector series, and more. The univariate ARIMA model is of the linear type and is applied to data that is predominantly linear in nature. It is expressed by a global formula with fixed coefficients, calculated for the data used, which is valid for each moment in time t. The standard notation for the model is set as ARIMA(p,d, q)$_S$. Here, the parameters p, d, q, s are non-negative integers and mean as follows:

- p – number of lagged variables of the dependent time series describing the deterministic part of the model. With their values, p coefficients of the model of a linear autoregressive process (AR) are determined to establish the influence of data from p previous moments in Y_t for each current t;
- d – order of integration (order of differentiation, number of trends), (I);
- q – number of stochastic terms participating in the model for smoothing small fluctuations using their linear combination, known as moving average (MA) process for each t;
- s – number of seasonality lags: 12 for months in a year, 7 – number of days in a week, 24 – number of hours in a day, etc.

The algorithm for building an ARIMA model is an iterative process for step-by-step calculation of the values of the coefficients of the model with initially set p, d, q, s. It first checks for a trend and if there are trends (i.e., if $d > 0$), these are removed to obtain a stationary series. At the next stages, the estimates and statistical significance of the remaining coefficients are calculated. This is achieved by iterative procedures for minimizing the sum of the squares of the deviations, which is a standard loss function [1-3].

It is accepted when modeling time series to divide the initial sample into several parts. For example, one part is used to build the model and find its coefficients, and other parts are used for test and verification. In the test sample, the values of the target variable are removed to be predicted by the model. These are then compared to the original data to determine how well the model predicts unknown, say "unseen" data. The error of this prediction is called prediction error and is one of the criteria for selecting the final model.

The ARIMA algorithm and its variants are implemented in many statistical software packages, for example, in SPSS, Wolfram Mathematica, etc.

- Theoretical assumptions for applying ARIMA

Each method has certain requirements and assumptions for its use. For a statistically valid ARIMA model, the minimum conditions are that the data have a normal or close to normal distribution; possibility of initial bringing to stationary series; linear or close to linear character of the studied time series; model errors should not contain autocorrelations and others [1-3]. These requirements are checked before constructing the model. In the process of generating the model, the significance of its coefficients is monitored. An important point for obtaining an adequate model, capable of predicting new values well, is the analysis and diagnosis of its residuals (errors), and it is also checked whether there is a lack of autocorrelation in them, etc. [3, 4].

The standard computational procedure for generating a univariate ARIMA model includes the following main steps, which are applied iteratively:

- Initial processing of the data and checks of the requirements for applying the method;
- Identification - research to determine tentative values of the parameters p, d, q, s;
- Calculation and evaluation of model coefficients;
- Research on residuals;
- Model selection;
- Application of the selected ARIMA model.

Let Y_t are the values of the time series (pollutant) at time *t*, and *B* is the lag operator that indicates the previous observation for each *t* , i.e.

$$BY_t = Y_{t-1}. \tag{3.1}$$

A stationary time series describes a deterministic autoregressive AR process of order p if it satisfies a finite difference equation of order p of the form:

$$Y_t = \phi_1 Y_{t-1} + \phi_2 Y_{t-2} + \ldots + \phi_p Y_{t-p} + a_t = \left(\sum_{j=1}^{p} \phi_j B^j\right) Y_t + a_t,$$
$$t = p+1, \ldots, N, \tag{3.2}$$

where $(\phi_1, \phi_2, \ldots, \phi_p)$ are constant coefficients (model parameters), a_t is a stochastic component (random error, white noise) for each time *t*, under the assumption $a_t \sim WN(0, \sigma^2)$. We will note that the AR model with equation (3.2) has the form of a regression equation for the variable Y, which depends on its values in the previous p moments (which is the autoregression).

Let us now consider a process of systematic random fluctuations around a certain fundamental level. In this case, each current value Y_t can be considered as a stochastic MA process influenced by white noise a_t. A moving average MA model is of order q if, for each *t*, it satisfies a finite difference equation of order q:

$$Y_t = a_t - \theta_1 a_{t-1} - \theta_2 a_{t-2} - \ldots - \theta_q a_{t-q} = \left(1 - \sum_{j=1}^{q} \theta_j B^j\right) a_t, \quad t = q+1, \ldots, N, \tag{3.3}$$

where $\theta_1, \theta_2, \ldots, \theta_q$ are constant coefficients.

In the general case, the series may not be stationary and a deterministic trend of some order (linear, quadratic, etc. up to order d) may be present in it. The transition to a stationary time series requires the precomputation of an appropriate number of finite differences of the series with a $(1 - B)^d$ stationarity-type operator. For example, a first-order trend is a first order finite difference, calculated by subtracting the previous value from each current time series value, i.e.:

$$trend_1 Y_t = Y_t - Y_{t-1}, \quad t = 2,3, \ldots, N. \tag{3.4}$$

For a non-stationary time, series *Y* with an autoregressive (AR) process and accounting for stochastic fluctuations with an MA process, the general form of an ARIMA (p , d , q) model is written as

$$\left(1 - \sum_{j=1}^{p} \phi_j B^j\right)(1 - B)^d Y_t = \left(1 - \sum_{j=1}^{q} \theta_j B^j\right) a_t + c, \tag{3.5}$$

where *c* is a constant. Denoting the finite difference operator by $\nabla B = 1 - B$, the ARIMA model (3.5) takes the form:

$$\phi_p(B) \nabla^d Y_t = \theta_q(B) a_t + c, \tag{3.6}$$

where $\phi_p(B)$, $\theta_q(B)$ are the difference polynomials from (3.5)

$$\phi_p(B) = \left(1 - \sum_{j=1}^{p} \phi_j B^j\right), \quad \theta_q(B) = \left(1 - \sum_{j=1}^{q} \theta_j B^j\right).$$

Oftentimes, series are observed to have seasonality or periodicity in time with a fixed durations s. In this case, a seasonal variant of the ARIMA process called SARIMA can be used. It is formulated with parameters (P , D , Q) with a similar meaning as in ARIMA and a seventh parameter is set for the lag - s . The notation is SARIMA (p, d, q) (P, D, Q)$_s$, where P is the number of parameters for the seasonal autoregression (SAR), D is the order of the seasonal finite difference, Q is the number of terms in the seasonal moving average process (SMA). In the seasonal part of the model, these three parameters are used with lag s. In all cases where there is a trend, the ARIMA/SARIMA model should not include the constant *c*, which is dropped when calculating a finite difference of the time series.

The general form of a multiplicative SARIMA model is

$$\begin{aligned}&\phi_p(B)\Phi_P(B^s)\nabla^d\nabla_s^D Y_t = \theta_q(B)\Theta_Q(B^s)a_t + c,\\ &\nabla_s^D = (1-B^s)^D, \quad a_t \sim WN(0,\sigma^2),\end{aligned} \tag{3.7}$$

where $\phi_p(B), \Phi_P(B^s), \theta_q(B), \Theta_Q(B^s)$ are finite difference polynomials.

For example, the model SARIMA (1,1,1)(0,1,1)$_{24}$ is written as $(1-\phi_1 B)\nabla\nabla_{24}Y_t = (1-\theta_1 B)(1-\Theta_{24}B^{24})a_t$ or in finite difference equation form

$$\begin{aligned}&(1-\phi_1 B)(1-B)(1-B^{24})Y_t = Y_t - (1+\phi_1)Y_{t-1} + \phi_1 Y_{t-2} - Y_{t-24}\\ &+(1+\phi_1)Y_{t-25} - \phi_1 Y_{t-26} = a_t - \theta_1 a_{t-1} - \Theta_{24}a_{t-24} + \theta_1\Theta_{24}a_{t-25}.\end{aligned} \tag{3.8}$$

The model (3.8) accounts for the time series dependence of Y for each current value Y_t on its values at the previous two moments and one term with 24-time moments back, as well as noise-smoothing values on the right-hand side of (3.8). With known values of Y_t up to t -1, if we ignore the unknown value a_t, the model gives the following prediction $\hat{Y}_t$ for Y_t

$$\begin{aligned}\hat{Y}_t = &(1+\phi_1)Y_{t-1} - \phi_1 Y_{t-2} + Y_{t-24} - (1+\phi_1)Y_{t-25} + \phi_1 Y_{t-26}\\ &-\theta_1 a_{t-1} - \Theta_{24}a_{t-24} + \theta_1\Theta_{24}a_{t-25}.\end{aligned} \tag{3.9}$$

We will note that obviously any SARIMA process (3.7) can be reduced to the general form of an ARMA process. By expanding the polynomials on both sides of (3.7) we will obtain an ARMA(p+sP+d+sD, q+sQ) model. Also, an ARIMA process (3.5) can be written as ARMA (p+d, q). This equivalence is automated in some software packages, e.g., in Wolfram Mathematica, Time series package (see [4]).

- Identification and selection of ARIMA model parameters

As mentioned, after initial data preparation, the time series is checked for stationarity and the value of the parameter *d* is determined. For this purpose, the Augmented Dickey-Fuller (ADF) test could be applied to the processed data [5] or another statistical test for the presence of a unit root. This statistical approach is suitable for larger and more complex sets of time series models and is applicable even for models with an unknown degree of trend. The results of the unit root test depend on the chosen significance level (most often it is $\alpha = 0.05$).

Usually, to determine the parameters p, q, the empirical autocorrelation function (ACF) and the partial autocorrelation function (PACF) are analyzed. The ACF and PACF distributions show the behavior and suggest the possible higher parameters for AR and MA processes in the model. Determination of parameters, seasonality, autoregression, moving average process, etc. is described in most detail in [4].

- Some guidelines for choosing ARIMA model parameters

When a set of strict constraints (control parameters) is set to the methods, it is possible to obtain a single solution. In the cases we consider, this almost never ensures obtaining the "best" (in the sense of the best fit to the data) model. The reason is that the model evaluation criteria are generally contradictory. For example, if we are looking for a model with the highest coefficient of determination R^2, then it will certainly be overdetermined, because in nested models with an increase in the number of parameters, R^2 also grows. It should be noted in particular that the coefficient of determination is correlation-based, with the resulting limitations on its interpretation [6]. By setting more general constraints, a class of solutions is obtained, possibly on the order of tens of solutions. This is not a disadvantage. Oftentimes, the number of control parameters for an "optimal model" can be justified using more objective information criteria such as Akaike Information Criterion AIC [7], Bayesian Information Criterion (BIC) [8], or others [9].

Practice has established the opinion that the normalized BIC criterion should be used out of the information criteria. Its value is easily calculated by the expression

$$BIC = \ln\left(\sum_{t=1}^{N}\left(Y_t - \hat{Y}_t\right)^2 / (N - m)\right) + \frac{m\, ln(N)}{N}, \tag{3.10}$$

where m is the total number of model parameters. Among the preferred models are those with the minimum BIC value. It should be noted that this criterion derives from various assumptions, including a normal or near-normal distribution of the data [10], which is an assumption for building ARIMA models.

We will also note that only nested models can be compared with information criteria, without intermediate data transformations or models built with completely different methods [11].

In addition to the normalized BIC criterion (3.10), when choosing a model, statistics are also used to evaluate the approximation of the model to the data. The accuracy of the model is established by appropriate model-performance measures. The main ones are given in Chapter 2, formulas (2.12)-(2.16). In addition to these, the diagnosis of the distribution of model residuals, the ACF study to check the absence of serial correlation in them, statistical tests, and other appropriate tools should not be neglected [12, 13]. After building a model, its predictive quality is also evaluated for the cases from the test sample that did not participate in building the model itself. A model is chosen that shows a good prognostic quality. When more models show close statistics with the best values according to the criteria, a parsimonious model is selected [1].

The model is considered adequate and statistically acceptable if its residuals are small, randomly distributed and do not contain autocorrelations. If a model is not satisfactory, the process is repeated, but with changed parameters p, d, q, s. This procedure is repeated until a satisfactory model is found. From this point on, the model found can be used for predictive purposes.

3.2.2. Wavelet Transform

The foundations of wavelet transform (WT) theory were developed in the classic works of Mallat and Daubechies [14, 15], providing rich tools for time–frequency analysis. WT is considered as an analogue and a generalization of Fourier transform.

Graphically, wavelets are short-lived wavelike oscillations whose amplitude starts at zero increases and decreases back to zero. They are generated using some type of wavelet mother function $\psi(t)$ or "small wave," defined in a short interval. With a parameterization of this function, a given time series function or signal $f(t)$ is decomposed. As a result, $f(t)$ is presented as a linear sum of a set of components that represent trend, seasonality, amplitudes and other characteristics, as well as noise inherent in most empirical time series. In this way, local time-varying periods and intensities of the time series behavior are taken into account [14-17].

Wavelet decomposition, however, is performed within the domain of definition of $f(t)$. To build models capable of predicting beyond this interval, various methods such as ARIMA, Artificial neural networks (ANN), deep learning, or other ML predictive methods and techniques are applied to the decomposed components obtained as a result of WT. In some cases, this hybrid approach improves prediction, but in others it may not be successful enough [18].

WT can be continuous or discrete type, denoted by CWT and DWT, respectively. Let some wavelet function $\psi(t)$ be selected. In the continuous case, it is parameterized in the form [16]

$$\psi_{a,b}(t) = \frac{1}{\sqrt{|a|}}\psi\left(\frac{t-b}{a}\right), \tag{3.11}$$

under the conditions

$$\int_0^{\infty} \frac{|\psi(t)|}{t} dt < \infty, .. \tag{3.12}$$

$$\int_{-\infty}^{\infty} |\psi(t)|^2 \, dt = 1 \, . \tag{3.13}$$

Here "a" is a scaling parameter, "b" is a location (or position) parameter. Using (3.11), the WT is defined for any function $f(t)$ in the Hilbert space $L^2(\mathbb{R})$ as:

$$W(a,b) = \int_t f(t) \frac{1}{\sqrt{|a|}} \psi\left(\frac{t-b}{a}\right) dt, \quad f(t) \in L^2(\mathbb{R}). \tag{3.14}$$

For each a and b, the corresponding wavelet transform coefficient is calculated, which approximates $f(t)$ at location $t = a/b$. To switch to an orthonormal basis and reduce the number of coefficients, (3.14) is used with a special selection of a and b, by introducing two integer parameters j and k. For $a = 2^{-j}$, $W(a,b)$ from (3.14) takes the form:

$$W(j,k) = \int f(t)\, \psi_{j,k}(t) dt, \tag{3.15}$$

where the wavelet coefficients are

$$\psi_{j,k}(t) = 2^{j/2}\psi(2^j t - k). \quad (3.16)$$

Well-known continuous wavelet families are Mexican hat, Gabor wavelet, Gaussian wavelet, Morlet wavelet, etc. [16].

In the case of real-world problems, it is often more appropriate to use a discrete analogue of the WT, or DWT. Depending on the type of known values of $f(t)$, a suitable wavelet is chosen. Performing the decomposition the DWT coefficients are calculated. The general form of decomposition is

$$f(t) = \sum_{k\in\mathbb{Z}} c_{o,k}\phi_{o,k}(t) + \sum_{j=0}^{\infty}\sum_{k\in\mathbb{Z}} d_{j,k}\psi_{j,k}(t), \quad (3.17)$$

$$c_{j,k}(f) =< f, \phi_{j,k} >= \int f(t)\, \phi_{j,k}(t)dt, \quad (3.18)$$

$$d_{j,k}(f) =< f, \psi_{j,k} >= \int f(t)\, \psi_{j,k}(t)dt, \quad (3.19)$$

where $\phi_{j,k}(t)$ are the corresponding scaling functions and $\psi_{j,k}(t)$ are the wavelet functions. The functions $\psi_{j,k}(t)$ are calculated from the mother wavelet using the expression

$$\psi_{j,k} = 2^{\frac{j}{2}}\psi(2^j t - k). \quad (3.20)$$

After decomposing $f(t)$ the resulting components are transformed with a corresponding inverse DWT and can be modelled with predictive methods.

Some of the popular WT families are biorthogonal splines, Daubechies, and Haar wavelets [16]. Examples of their mother wavelets are shown in Figure 3.2.

The DWT process converts a given signal into a simple sum of a basic low-frequency signals, called the Approximations or Coarse signals (Aj), and high-frequency details or refinements (Dj) with respect to time. In the inverse transform, any part of the decomposition can be separated out to reduce noise or any other part of interest. To obtain a decomposition with a finite number of components in (3.17), the number of extracted refinements *j* is set, which is equal to the current highest index of the approximation component Aj.

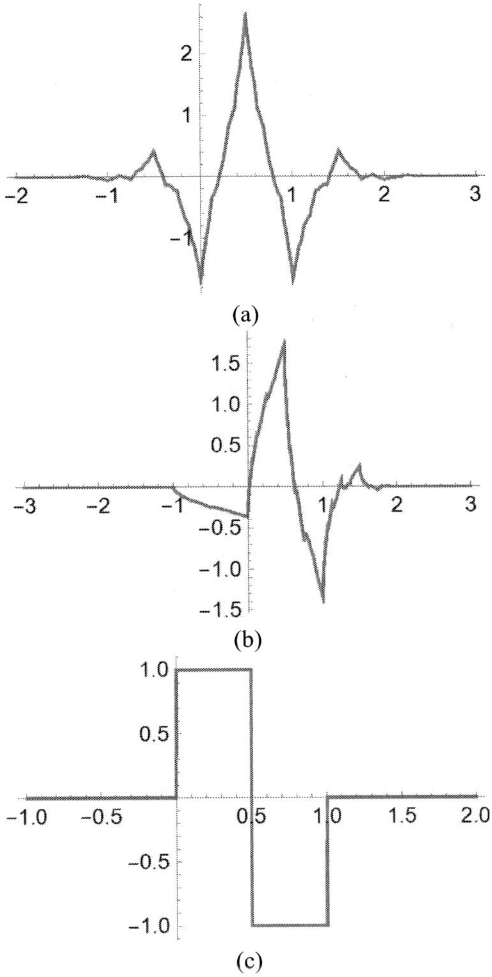

Figure 3.2. Plots of the wavelet functions $\psi(t)$ for: (a) Biorthogonal splines wavelet of order 2 and dual order 4 (B); (b) Daubechies wavelet of order 2 (D); (c) Haar (H).

A process of DWT decomposition of a signal (or data) in the form of a tree is shown in Figure 3.3 for a case with the third approximation component A3 and three details D1, D2, D3. The decomposition is presented as a sum Signal=A3+D1+D2+D3. The process proceeds as at each step the current approximation signal is divided into low frequency and high frequency components, and additional coarse and detail terms are determined.

The following Figure 3.4 shows an example of the result of DWT decomposition with B-splines with 4 details 1,2,3,4 and approximation A4 (A4 is the last plot on the right).

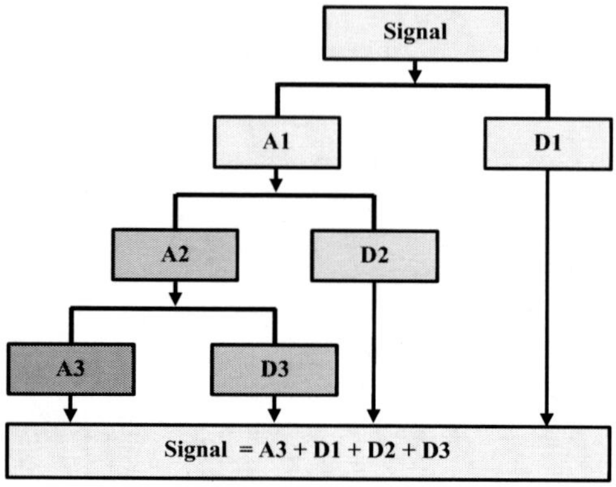

Figure 3.3. Tree form of the decomposition process of the initial signal with three refinements in the sum of the approximation part and the details in DWT.

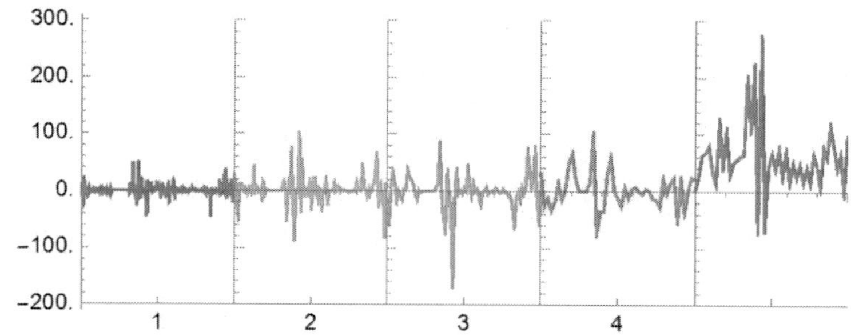

Figure 3.4. Example of signal decomposition with B-splines DWT with 4 details 1,2,3,4 and approximation A4 (right) on the common scale.

The conditions, properties, types of CWT and DWT, their inverse transformations and properties are presented in theoretical papers (see [16, 17]).

- Some practical aspects of the application of DWT

When DWT is used to separate a characteristic trend from the decomposition, the approximation component Aj is used, and to reduce noise in the data - the first few detail components.

There are different approaches in the literature for choosing the index j of Aj. From these, the simplest is the following rule [19]:

$$\frac{\text{Std.}\,Dev.(\text{Aj})}{\text{Std.}\,Dev.(Y)} \leq 0.1, \tag{3.21}$$

where Std.Dev. is the standard deviation, calculated for the time series Aj and the initial data Y, respectively. The number of details j increases until (3.21) is satisfied.

A key element in DWT is the ability to select a threshold value δ and the threshold function of the inverse transform, so as to control the number of decomposition coefficients and more accurately filter the time series or signal. Different approaches are used in the literature to determine δ, see for instance, [20].

A frequently used criterion is Donoho and Johnstone's universal threshold [20, 21]. It is calculated using the "hard" threshold function according to the expression

$$\delta = \sigma_{MAD}\sqrt{2\text{Log}_{10}(N)}, \tag{3.22}$$

$$\sigma_{MAD} = \frac{\text{MAD(D1)}}{0.67449}, \tag{3.23}$$

where MAD is the mean absolute deviation, computed using detail coefficients at the first refinement level D1. Another option for choosing δ is to apply (3.22) - (3.23) to all refinement levels, not only to D1. It is possible to choose different threshold functions, as shown below.

Close to this threshold choice δ is the expression

$$\delta = \sigma_2\sqrt{2\text{Log}(N)}, \tag{3.24}$$

where σ_2 is an estimate of the standard deviation of the noise (see [22], p. 180).

Another empirical way to find an acceptable value of δ is its empirical determination. Several thresholds

$$\delta_k = \frac{\text{Std.Dev.(Aj)}}{k} \tag{3.25}$$

are calculated for different k and the distribution of the residuals $\varepsilon = Y - \mathrm{Aj}$ is examined until it becomes close to a standard Gaussian white noise.

Some software packages offer automatic threshold value estimation (for instance, in Wolfram Mathematica).

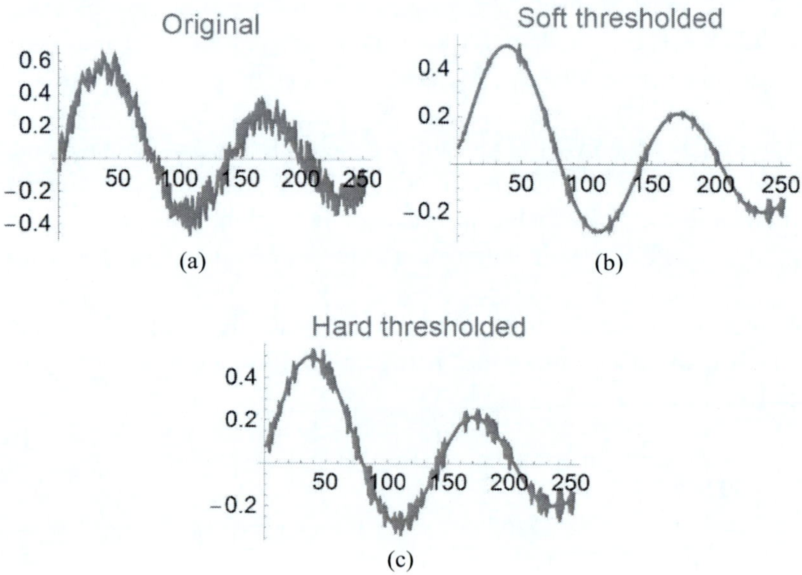

Figure 3.5. Examples of data denoising using Soft and Hard thresholding functions with the same universal thresholding value.

Table 3.1. Basic thresholding functions in wavelet analysis

Thresholding function	Formulas
Hard	$Hard\_tr(\delta) = \begin{cases} 0 & \text{at } \lvert x\rvert \le \delta \\ x & \text{at } \lvert x\rvert > \delta \end{cases}$
Soft	$Soft\_tr(\delta) = \begin{cases} 0 & \text{at } \lvert x\rvert \le \delta \\ \mathrm{Sgn}(x)(\lvert x\rvert - \delta) & \text{at } \lvert x\rvert > \delta \end{cases}$
Piecewise Garrote	$PwGarrote\_tr(\delta) = \begin{cases} 0 & \text{at } \lvert x\rvert \le \delta \\ x - \frac{\delta^2}{x} & \text{at } \lvert x\rvert > \delta \end{cases}$
Hyperbola	$Hyp\_tr(\delta) = \begin{cases} 0 & \text{at } \lvert x\rvert \le \delta \\ \mathrm{Sgn}(x)\sqrt{x^2 - \delta^2} & \text{at } \lvert x\rvert > \delta \end{cases}$

The chosen wavelet threshold δ is a parameter of various thresholding functions for cancellation of decomposition coefficients. It applies primarily to details of DWT or to all derived components. There is extensive literature in the field of wavelet analysis and wavelet thresholding, including time series applications [23-26].

Table 3.1 presents some of the most commonly used thresholding functions that have different effects on noise removal. Examples of signal denoising are shown in Figure 3.5.

3.2.3. Temporal Causal Modeling (TCM)

Temporal causal modelling (TCM) is a statistical approach based on the Granger causality test [27, 28, Ch 17.4]. It attempts to discover key causal relationships in vector time series data. This approach differs from traditional time series modeling, where you must explicitly specify the predictors for a target series. Since TCM typically involves building models for multiple related time series, the result is referred to as a model system.

Unlike static data, for time series, the following assumption implies: "If event A happens before event B, then it is possible that A is causing B. However, it is not possible that B is causing A. In other words, events in the past can cause events to happen today. Future events cannot" [29].

Following this logic, the Granger causality test is used to test causality (but not cause-and-effect) between several time series. The idea of the test consists in the assumption that the values of a given time series $\{X_t\}$ significantly affect the changes and forecasting of another series $\{Y_t\}$. The opposite is also possible, i.e., $\{Y_t\}$ to have a major significance on the prediction of $\{X_t\}$. In this case, there may be a third series that affects both of these at the same time. The Granger causality test successively checks the following two hypotheses:

" $\{X_t\}$ is not a Granger cause of $\{Y_t\}$ ",
" $\{Y_t\}$ is not a Granger cause of $\{X_t\}$ ".

Intuitively, for a strictly stationary bivariate process $\{(X_t, Y_t)\}$ a variable $\{X_t\}$ is a Granger cause of $\{Y_t\}$ if past and current values of X contain additional information on future values of Y that is not contained in past and current Y-values alone [30].

The Granger causality assumes that the variables $\{X_t\}, \{Y_t\}$ are stationary and follow the normal distribution. In the TCM applications, the series of the lagged terms used their number can vary. All coefficients of the model are checked for significance and only those with p-value less than α (usually $\alpha = 0.05$ are retained. In addition, one should be aware that TCM is sensitive to the inclusion of lagged variables [28, Ch. 17.4].

In order to achieve the prescribed assumptions, before applying the TCM with the Granger causality test, it is often necessary to transform the variables and bring them into stationary series. In our considerations, TCM is implemented using SPSS statistical software [31].

In the simplest case, let us assume two stationary time series, $X = \{X_1, X_2, \dots, X_t, \dots, X_N\}$ and $Y = \{Y_1, Y_2, \dots, Y_t, \dots, Y_N\}$ with values at the same time points $t, t = 1,2,\dots,N$. We consider the symmetric autoregressive processes of order q:

$$\begin{aligned} Y &= a_0 + \textstyle\sum_{k=1}^{q} a_k Y_{t-k} + \sum_{k=1}^{q} b_k X_{t-k} + \varepsilon_t, \qquad \varepsilon_t \in N(0, \sigma_1^2), \\ X_t &= c_0 + \textstyle\sum_{k=1}^{q} c_k X_{t-k} + \sum_{k=1}^{q} d_k X_{t-k} + \delta_{t,} \qquad \delta_t \in N(0, \sigma_2^2), \end{aligned} \tag{3.26}$$

where $t = q+1, \dots, N,\ a_0, a_k, b_k, c_0, c_k, d_k,\ k = 0,1,\dots,q$ are constant coefficients, q is the number of lags.

The Granger test examines the following two null hypotheses sequentially:

$$H_0^{(Y)}: b_1 = b_2 = \dots = b_q = 0,\ H_0^{(X)}: d_1 = d_2 = \dots = d_q = 0. \tag{3.27}$$

In essence, the hypothesis $H_0^{(Y)}$ tests whether the time series X Granger cause Y, and reciprocally $H_0^{(X)}$ checks if Y Granger causes X. A statistically significant test result with a small p-value means that the null hypothesis is false and should be rejected. A p-value greater than α has come to refer to the "null" causal effect. Hypotheses (3.27) can be tested with the F-test, LM, or t-test on lagged values of X and Y. It should be noted that the result of the tests depends on the number of lags q.

In the multivariate case, let us have an m-dimensional time series matrix $X = \left(X^{(1)}, X^{(2)}, \dots, X^{(m)}\right)$ with $X^{(j)} = \left\{X_1^{(j)}, X_2^{(j)}, \dots, X_N^{(j)}\right\},\ j = 1,2,\dots,m.$

The SPSS module TCM implies that all these time series are stationary and standardized them before the analysis. The TCM explores the autoregressive process of the type

$$X_t^{(j)} = A_0 + A_1 X_{t-1}^{(j)} + \ldots, A_q X_{t-q}^{(j)} + \varepsilon_{X,t},$$
$$t = q+1, \ldots, N, \quad j = 1,2, \ldots, m, \tag{3.28}$$

where A_j are matrices of coefficients, $\varepsilon_{X,t}$ is a random error followed the standard normal distribution. The null hypothesis for the Granger causality test implies that the variable $X^{(j)}$ does not cause $X^{(i)}, i \neq j$ through the check $A_i = 0$. The TCM algorithm then builds an autoregressive time series model for each target $X^{(i)}$ and includes only those inputs that have a causal relationship with the target $X^{(j)}$. This is done for selected or all vectors from the matrix X at a given number of lags q. A valid TCM model can be further used to obtain predictive models that provide adequate predictions of future values not used in building the models.

3.3. Basic Machine Learning (ML) Methods

Intelligent statistical modeling methods are based on ML and are a fundamental approach in artificial intelligence (AI). They are classified into two large groups - supervised learning and unsupervised learning. Here we will mainly use the first type of methods. The main classes of basic ML methods are summarized in our review of ML studies (see Chapter 1.1). From an empirical point of view, it is accepted that "some classification and regression methods are unstable in the sense that small perturbations in their training sets or in construction may result in large changes in the results of the constructed model. Subset selection methods in regression, decision trees in regression and classification, and neural nets are unstable" [32, 33]. At the same time, constructing combination of unstable models, such as ensembles, could yield to stable model, providing a dramatic decrease of the bias, variance and prediction (generalization) error [32].

In supervised learning, a given ML model is trained in different ways. The training is based on the idea that the model should gain experience in different situations and improve its results, simulating the human approach. For this purpose, as we mentioned, the data are divided into two parts - one part is left as a test, and the model itself is built and evaluated with the remaining part - a training (learning) sample. In the case of time series, the test sample usually includes time-sequential moments from the terminal part of the initial series. Training can be done in different ways.

An old statistical approach is the use of the generalized cross-validation criterion, originally proposed in [34]. In some methods such as Random Forest (RF), a subsample called out of bag (OOB) is randomly selected from the training sample and used to test the rest of the training sample. Another widely applied technique is the V-fold cross-validation [35, p. 12].

- V-fold cross-validation procedure

The training sample L is randomly divided into V non-overlapping subsamples of approximately equal volume $L_1, L_2, ..., L_V$. Of these, the union of (V-1) subsets is used to build the model (learn sample), and the rest – for testing (test sample). This learning process is repeated V times for each sample combination. The process is shown in Figure 3.6 for the case V=5.

Test 1	Learn	Learn	Learn	Learn
Learn	Test 2	Learn	Learn	Learn
Learn	Learn	Test 3	Learn	Learn
Learn	Learn	Learn	Test 4	Learn
Learn	Learn	Learn	Learn	Test 5

Figure 3.6. Example of data splitting in a 5-fold cross-validation procedure.

The variant with the lowest root-mean-square error, or other selected measure of accuracy, is selected as the final model. By applying the chosen algorithm with separate test samples, cross-validation provides a more realistic estimate of the model's ability to approximate "new" data.

In practice, the use of a 10-fold CV is prevalent. From now on, we will adopt this option as the standard.

3.3.1. Classification and Regression Trees (CART)

This method is fundamental in the group of decision tree learning. Decision trees provide powerful ML and data mining tools used in medicine, economy, ecology, and many other areas [36, 35, 22]. Another popular variant of the CART algorithm is C4.5 [37].

Generally, CART is a supervised learning algorithm for classification and regression problems. It is capable to process very large or small datasets and arbitrary type of variables. Like most ML methods, CART is distribution free, meaning that no specific conditions are placed on the type of probabilistic distributions of the variables. CART can handle locally linear, nonlinear effects and interaction terms in a hierarchical rule sequence.

Among the advantages of the CART method are also simplicity and easy interpretation, due to the "white box" model, in which an explicit binary rule is generated for each splitting of the sample and the contribution to the improvement of the model is calculated; robust statistical method, insensitive to outlying cases, requires little preliminary data preparation, automatic selection of model variables, etc.

- CART algorithm for regression

The CART algorithm is based on a recursive type partitioning of the initial dataset into non-overlapping multidimensional sub-regions (classes). This is done in two successive steps - forward and backward. The forward stage results in an unpruned maximal tree and the backward stage results in removing nonredundant branches and nodes of the tree [35, 36].

In the forward step, the initial learning sample with data of the target variable Y_t is recursively divided into non-intersecting parts called nodes in the form of a binary tree. By means of hyperparameters, the growth of the tree is stopped. In this way, the output dataset of *Y's* is distributed in the terminal nodes (leaves) of the tree.

The predicted values $\hat{Y}_t$ of Y_t of the model are calculated as the arithmetic mean of the cases classified at the terminal nodes of the tree. Basic hyperparameters for model tuning are: minimum number of observations in a parent and child node, type of classification method (usually Gini), error function (mean squared error (MSE), least absolute deviation), validation method (unvalidated (or unpruned maximal) tree, cross-validation, validation with external testing), etc.

The splitting of the data from each node of the tree is carried out with the extensive greedy algorithm. For all possible values of each of the independent variables for the cases from the node, a minimum of a selected error criterion is sought. Most commonly, this is the MSE of the current model. Let the minimum be reached for a value $X_{ij} \in X_i$. It is called the threshold value for the current node and is denoted by θ_i. The splitting of the cases from the node into two new hereditary (child) nodes is done according to the rule:

$$\text{"If } X_{ij} \leq \theta_i\text{, then } Y_j \text{ is classified in a left child node,} \\ \text{else } Y_j \text{ is classified in a right child node."} \tag{3.29}$$

In the backward step of the CART algorithm, branches that do not significantly improve the model's accuracy can be pruned. The prediction of new values not used for CART at known values of the independent variables is obtained by sequentially applying the rule (3.29), starting from the root of the tree [36, 35, 38].

We will briefly illustrate the method with an example using the data from Table 3.2. This table contains 15 values of two independent variables X1, X2, and a dependent variable *Y*. The task is to predict *Y* using CART.

A variant of a CART tree with four terminal nodes is shown in Figure 3.7. The threshold values at each splitting of a node are given as inequalities of type (3.29). At the first level, node 1 contains all 15 *Y* values. The predicted value of the model at this node is the average of the contained values, equal to Avr = 24.2. At this point, the model mean squared error by formula (2.13) is

$$MSE = \frac{1}{N}\sum_{j=1}^{N}(Y_j - P_j)^2 = \frac{1}{15}\sum_{j=1}^{15}(Y_j - 24.2)^2 = \frac{2168.4}{15} = 144.56.$$

Table 3.2. Example data for Figure 3.7

Index	X1	X2	Y
1	1	3	6
2	1	4	7
3	-2	6	10
4	3	7	20
5	4	9	45
6	2	9	25
7	3	5	20
8	5	6	37
9	2	6	15
10	3	7	30
11	4	8	40
12	5	5	30
13	3	6	20
14	2	7	18
15	4	9	40

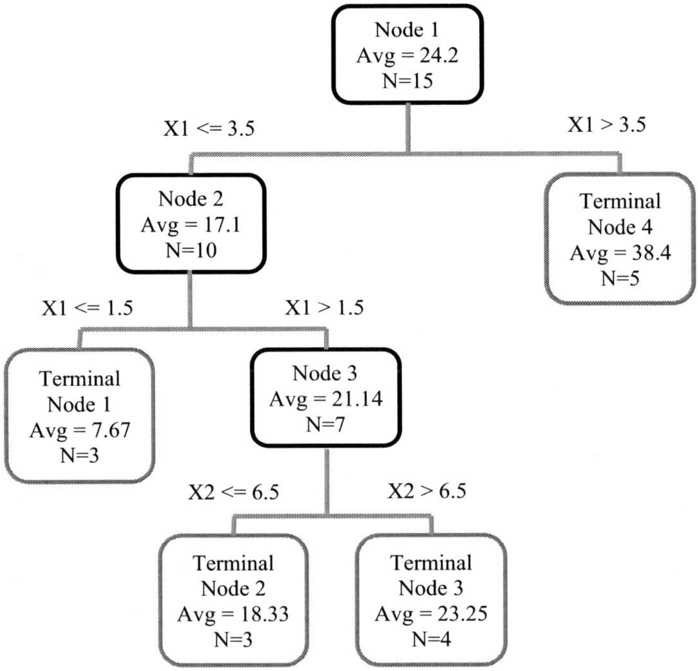

Figure 3.7. An example of generating a CART tree with two independent variables.

In the next step, the CART algorithm calculates all possible errors for splitting the values from node 1 by trying all candidates for a threshold value of 15 values for X1 and X2. This is how the threshold value $\theta_1 = 3.5$ for the variable X1 between 3 and 4 is obtained, which yields the smallest MSE. The result of splitting by (3.29) is two subsets of *Y* in nodes 2 and 4 with 10 and 5 observations, respectively. The predicted values in these nodes are 17.1 for node 2 and 38.4 for node 4. Further, the algorithm continues similarly by dividing the values in these two nodes, and so on. For example, according to Figure 3.7 and selecting values X1=2, X2=9, this case will be classified through nodes 1, 2, 3 in terminal node 3. The corresponding predicted value will be the average value of the observations in node 3, equal to $\hat{Y}(2.9) = 23.25$. The exact value is 25.

In ML, the model's performance is evaluated not only for its overall accuracy, but rather for its prediction accuracy for some known test sample of data that were not used in building the model. Usually, when selecting the best pruned subtree in CART to avoid overfitting the model, a learning procedure with a cross-validation is used. For small samples (with less than 10,000 observations), the standard 10-fold cross-validation is recommended [36, 38, 35] (see also Figure 3.6).

Depending on the research method and the source data, different regression trees can be built with the described original CART algorithm or with its variants. The choice of the best final model is determined by the researcher.

Decision trees also have some disadvantages. In general, it is considered that CART models are unstable, meaning that a small change in the data can result in a large change in the structure of the optimal decision tree. Another possible disadvantage is the possibility of obtaining a biased model when many categorical variables with different numbers of distinct categories are used [39].

However, as we have shown in our publication [40], these shortcomings can be significantly reduced by calibrating CART models using suitable cross-validation, specialized pruning procedures, variable grouping, and more.

- CART model selection and evaluation

Depending on the software used to generate CART models, a single optimal model can be obtained for given control parameters. This does not always result in the best model describing our data. The accuracy of predicting the test sample is also important here. The reason lies in the well-known fact that the model evaluation criteria are controversial [9]. For example, if we are looking for a model with the highest coefficient of determination, it will certainly be determined as the best, because as the number of parameters in the model increases, this coefficient increases. In other cases, setting more general constraints will yield a whole class of tentative optimal models, possibly of the order of tens and hundreds of solutions. This is not a disadvantage, but it allows the researcher to choose among them the most suitable model for the data under study.

In practice, when the obtained tentative best models from a given class with given variables and control settings are evaluated, they are normally evaluated with several popular goodness-of-fit statistical criteria, such as the root mean square error (RMSE), MSE, coefficient of determination, contingency tables, ROC curves, etc. For the candidate best CART models, models with the smallest RMSE, the highest coefficient of determination R^2 within one standard error (1 - SE rule) from the optimal model will be preferred [40]. These statistics should be considered simultaneously for learning and test samples. Moreover, in the case of a regression problem, there are different strategies for choosing the size of the tree [38, 35]. Practically, avoiding excessive complexity, every tree of the 1-SE set is still just as accurate and acceptable [40].

- Error diagnostics of a CART model

Similar to the ARIMA method described in 3.2.1, in the case of time series, the important stage of CART model error diagnostics cannot be omitted. The common assumptions for validating the regression model of the time series require that there is no serial correlation in the residuals of the model. However, the authors of [40, 41] argue that "in fact, there is currently no general diagnostic statistics for nonlinear autocorrelation relationships." This is particularly true for non-linear models with the lagged series of the variables used. However, in such a case, the Ljung-Box portfolio [42] and other similar statistics, which are valid for the assumption of linearity, cannot be used [43].

For non-linear time series models, it is recommended to analyze the ACF of their residuals

$$\varepsilon = Y - \hat{Y} , \tag{3.30}$$

(see also (2.7)) where $\hat{Y}$ is the selected CART model [40, 43]. If the model residuals have large deviations beyond the confidence limits of the ACF, we recommend smoothing the residuals ε by modeling them via an appropriate moving average process $\varepsilon = \text{MA}(q) + \hat{\varepsilon}$ [40]. This will result in an adjusted hybrid type CART-ARIMA error model

$$\tilde{Y} = \hat{Y} + MA(q) \tag{3.31}$$

with error term $\tilde{\varepsilon} = Y - \tilde{Y}$, assumed to be white noise.

Finally, if the selected fitted model passes the required accuracy and residual diagnostic tests, it can be considered adequate and is suitable for forecasting. In a real situation, however, it is necessary to know the values of the predictors for this process.

3.3.2. Multivariate Adaptive Regression Splines (MARS)

The mathematical foundations of MARS were developed by the American statistician Jerome Friedman in 1991 in [44]. The algorithms created by Friedman and their implementation are embedded in Salford Systems' MARS software [45, 46]. The method is also implemented in many other statistical packages: R, S-Plus, Statistica, etc.

MARS is representative of non-parametric ML methods, and can be classified as partial-polynomial regression in contrast to global classical regressions.

As a non-parametric regression method, MARS, unlike classical parametric regression techniques, does not place strong restrictions on the distributions of the data. For example, a multivariate normal distribution is not required. The method can be compared with other non-parametric methods for describing complex dependencies between variables, such as CART, ANN, additive models, in particular generalized additive models (GAM), and many others.

Some of the main advantages of MARS are:

- It can be used to model both quantitative and categorical data.
- Builds simple and easy-to-interpret ordinary linear regression-type models with partially continuous polynomial-type functions.
- Compared with CART, ANN, and other techniques, MARS is suitable for processing both large and small datasets (with a sample size of more than 50).
- Due to its simplicity, the implemented MARS algorithms run at a very high speed and enable the processing of huge data sets in real time (within 100 to 1000 times faster than ANN).

In essence, MARS creates flexible models through partial polynomial regressions using first-, second- and higher-degree polynomials. The non-linearities in the data are approximated by separate slopes in different subintervals of the definition set of each predictor variable. In the linear MARS model, instead of looking for a single general (global) regression line fitting the data, a broken line is used. The slope of the regression line changes from one interval to another in the so-called knots.

The knot is the main element of the model. It shows where the behavior of the function changes more sharply. In the classical spline, the knots are set in advance, while in MARS their most suitable place is found with a greedy forward algorithm for including only those tensor products that are deemed necessary by least squares [44, 22].

The other important elements in MARS are the basis functions (BFs), designed to transform the predictors. In the case of a linear model, dependent variable y and one predictor variable X, the basis function at node c has the form of a "hockey stick" and is set by one of the expressions

$$BF = max(0, X - c), \text{ or } BF = max(0, c - X). \tag{3.32}$$

A given predictor variable X can be converted to a set of BFs for different nodes. From (3.32), it can be seen that the basis function has only non-negative values, which helps the interpretation of the model.

In the multidimensional case, let the data be $\{y, X\} = \{Y_t, X_{1t}, X_{2t}, \dots, X_{pt}\}_{t=1}^{N}$. Here, y is the dependent variable and $\{X_1, X_2, \dots, X_p\}$ are the initial predictors.

The general form of the MARS model is

$$\hat{y}_{[M]}(X) = b_0 + \sum_{j=1}^{M} b_j BF_j(X), \tag{3.33}$$

where b_0, b_j are constant coefficients, M is a number of the BFs.

In the case of a nonlinear model, the basis functions $BF_j(X)$ may also contain a product of two or more functions of the form (3.32). A second-order basis function with an interaction between two predictors X_k and X_j is written as a product

$$BF_{k,j}(X) = max(0, X_k - c_{k,m_k})\, max(0, X_j - c_{j,m_j}), \quad k \neq j. \tag{3.34}$$

We note that the MARS model (3.33) differs from ordinary splines in that the nodes of the basis functions, the actual set of basis functions, and their number M are not known in advance. Instead, they are determined by additional optimization conditions, control hyperparameters, and constraints set by the researcher.

The algorithm for building MARS models proceeds in two steps: forward and backward. First, the maximum number of possible BFs (denoted by M_0) and the maximum order r of interaction between them (the maximum number of terms in a product of a BF) are set. After that, their number is at least doubled. It is recommended to fulfill the condition $M_0 \geq 3p$ [44, 46]. Limits can also be set on the size of the learning sample (Learn), the test sample (Test), for V-fold cross-validation order, and other additional restrictions.

The MARS algorithm starts with some value of the coefficient b_0 (for example $b_0 = \min_{1 \leq t \leq N} y_t$). Then, at each step in the model, a pair of mirror BFs of the type (3.32) or an analogous type with interaction up to order r is added for each variable. For a given intermediate model with L BFs, by default, the choice of variables, coefficients, and the corresponding number of nodes is determined by the condition to minimize the sum of squared errors (MSE)

$$SSE_{[L]} = \sum_{t=1}^{N} \left(y_t - \hat{y}_{[L]}(X_t)\right)^2. \tag{3.35}$$

As a result of the forward run, after computing all possible knot values and selecting the BFs, M_1 nested models are obtained. From this set of models, the best model has the smallest error (3.35) and the highest coefficient of determination R^2.

In the backward step, the contribution to the model accuracy of each member of the model is evaluated, and at each step, the one with the smallest contribution is removed. Backtracking evaluation in the MARS algorithm is performed using the generalized cross-validation criterion (GCV R^2) [44, 22]. A "best model" is selected from the $m = M$ members for which a minimum is reached of

$$GCV_{[m]}R^2 = \frac{\sum_{t=1}^{N} \left(y_t - \hat{y}_{[m]}(X_t)\right)^2}{N(1 - C(m)/N)^2}, \quad m = 1,2,\ldots,M_1, \tag{3.36}$$

where $C(m) = m + \delta(m-1)/2, \delta \in [2,3]$ [44]. The backward step allows for avoiding possible overfitting of the model. As a result, multiple models are obtained, including the so-called "best" model, with a minimum MARS GCV under the specified criteria and the preset hyperparameters at the beginning of the analysis.

We will note as an advantage of the MARS method the automatic selection of the essential predictors in the model and the determination of their individual contribution to the prediction of the dependent variable.

Depending on the purpose of statistical analysis, additional criteria for model selection could be set. Thus, the final model is selected by the researcher, whereby the "best" model suggested by the software used is not always preferred. We will call these criteria control hyperparameters. When building the models, some of these hyperparameters are necessarily set, for example, the maximum number of BFs in the model and the maximum order of interaction between the predictors. Other parameters are auxiliary and are set to specify the performance of the model, such as the size of subsets for cross-validation (V-fold), minimum number of observations between knots, speed of model generation, selection of grid for generating random samples for cross-validation, etc.

Detailed descriptions of the theoretical foundations of the MARS method and its capabilities can be found in a large number of publications, e.g., such as [44, 46]. Model selection is an important aspect of modeling, and in ML, it is based on cross-validation. The problem is addressed in numerous publications, e.g., [9, 35, 47, 48].

To illustrate MARS, we will use the data from Table 3.2, adding the results based on the constructed model (3.37) below. In the case of a linear model with a maximum of 7 basis functions (*BF*), the algorithm will obtain the following model:

$$BF1 = max(0, X1 + 2);$$
$$BF2 = max(0, X2 - 3);$$
$$BF3 = max(0, X1 + 0.784806);$$
$$YMARS = 0.446821 - 8.15528BF1 + 3.18437BF2 + 14.3729BF3. \quad (3.37)$$

Table 3.3. Example data and results to illustrate the MARS method

Index	*X*1	*X*2	*Y*	*BF*1 knots	*BF*2 knots	*BF*3 knots	*YMARS*
1	1	3	6	3	0	1.784806	1.63381916
2	1	4	7	3	1	1.784806	4.81818916
3	-2	6	10	0	3	0	9.999931
4	3	7	20	5	4	3.784806	26.8065392
5	4	9	45	6	6	4.784806	39.3928992
6	2	9	25	4	6	2.784806	26.9576592
7	3	5	20	5	2	3.784806	20.4377992
8	5	6	37	7	3	5.784806	36.0574092
9	2	6	15	4	3	2.784806	17.4045492
10	3	7	30	5	4	3.784806	26.8065392
11	4	8	40	6	5	4.784806	36.2085292
12	5	5	30	7	2	5.784806	32.8730392
13	3	6	20	5	3	3.784806	23.6221692
14	2	7	18	4	4	2.784806	20.5889192
15	4	9	40	6	6	4.784806	39.3928992

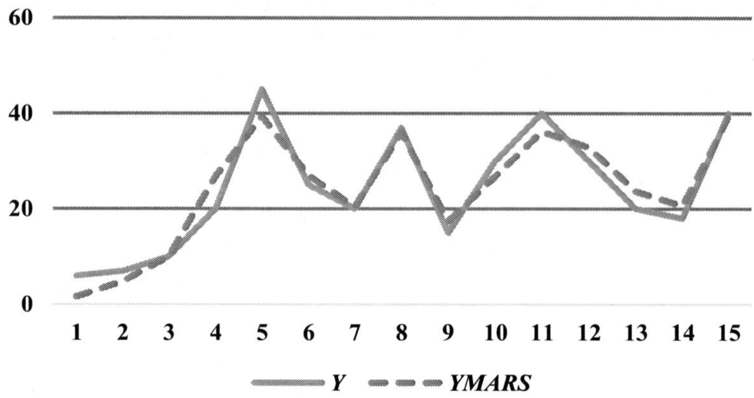

Figure 3.8. Example of a linear MARS model of the data from Table 3.3.

The calculations according to (3.37) are given in Table 3.3. The achieved approximation of the model to the values of *Y* is shown in Figure 3.8. Despite the simple appearance of the model, the approximation is very good.

In principle, regression splines, analogous to simple linear univariate regression, "average" the data that are grouped around the regression line. For this reason, when predicting results, especially at the boundaries of the multivariate region, the predicted values may be underestimated or overestimated with a positive or negative spline slope, respectively.

3.4. Ensemble Learning Methods

3.4.1. The Basis of Ensemble Learning and Bias-Variance Dilemma

In AI, ensemble learning is a major constituent of the ML paradigm. It applies in an automated way the "wisdom of the crowd," mainly referring to large groups of people, known as crowdsourcing (see [49]). The idea that a "crowd" can solve a problem or do a job better than an individual has been practiced for centuries in human history, dating back to the Tang dynasty of China (years 618-907).

Ensemble learning is a supervised approach in which a set of a finite number of models is trained to solve the same problem with the same algorithm. Combining their results yields the so-called ensemble model. It can solve a classification or regression problem. Ensembles are most often used with neural network algorithms or decision trees. Generally speaking, it is believed that a combination of several models outperforms a single "best" model [50, 51].

In applied statistics, the idea of combining forecasts dates back to the late 1970s. One of the first articles in this direction is the work of Bates and Granger from 1969 [52], in which monthly data on airline passenger miles flown are forecast. Predictions and one-month-ahead forecasts have been obtained using two different methods. Experiments were conducted combining their predictions with several different linear combinations using weights, including time-dependent weights. The combined models are shown to have smaller errors than the original two models. In fact, the presented "combination" of different models is rather a first attempt at stacking than an ensemble. In the work [53], the forecasts of two univariate time series are combined.

In recent years, ensemble learning has been intensively applied across various fields, with the development of AI methods [22, 54-57].

We consider a time series

$$Y = \{Y_t\}_{t=1}^{N} = \{y_1, y_2, \dots, y_t, \dots, y_N\}, \quad y_t \in \mathbb{R},$$

for which we seek an approximating series (model) of an arbitrary form

$$\begin{aligned} Y_t = f\big(&Y_{t-1}, \dots, Y_{t-p'}, X_{1,t}, \dots, X_{r,t}, \\ &X_{1,t-1}, \dots, X_{1,t-q_1'}, \dots, X_{r,t-1}, \dots, X_{r,t-q_r'}\big) + \varepsilon_t \end{aligned}$$

for known predictor series $X = (X_1, X_2, \dots, X_r)$. In reality, the initial sample Y belongs to a certain more general population, for which we are looking to establish statistical estimates and characteristics (average value, trend, etc.). The determination of the desired features can be approximated using newly formed samples from the original data. In practice, this is achieved, for example, by various redistributions of the data to create new sets of the same dimension by random subtraction with one or more data returned from the initial set Y, known as sampling with replacement [58]. This process is repeated many times. This way of data restructuring and redistribution is called bootstrap, and we will call the samples bootstrap-samples [22, 58].

Suppose that M models $f_j(X),\ j = 1,2,\dots,M$ of $Y(t)$ are generated each one using a different bootstrap sample.

Ensemble model $\bar{f}(X)$ of Y is called a linear combination of the type

$$\bar{f}(X) = \sum_{j=1}^{M} w_j f_j(X), \tag{3.38}$$

where w_j are weights, $0 < w_j \leq 1$, $j = 1,2,\ldots,M$, with a total sum of 1. Further, in the methods we use, all weights are equal, or $w_j = \frac{1}{M}$, $j = 1,2,,\ldots,M$. Therefore, such an ensemble model averages the predictions of its component single models, i.e.,

$$\bar{f}(X) = \frac{1}{M}\sum_{j=1}^{M} f_j(X). \tag{3.39}$$

The error of the ensemble is given by the expression

$$\varepsilon(X) = \left(Y(X) - \bar{f}(X)\right)^2 = \sum_{t=1}^{N}\left(Y(X_t) - \bar{f}(X_t)\right)^2. \tag{3.40}$$

When this type of error is examined only for the test sample, it is also called generalization error or prediction error [22, Ch. 3, pp. 37-38].

Another important measure of accuracy is the bias of the model, defined as

$$Bias(X) = \sum_{t=1}^{N}\left(Y(X_t) - \bar{f}(X_t)\right). \tag{3.41}$$

The generalized error and bias are mutually contradictory, since as the number M of members in the ensemble increases, the variance of the error grows and the bias decreases. A compromise is sought between them. This is known as the bias-variance dilemma. The following theorem is valid in the terminology of mathematical expectation (mean value) [59]. The decomposition for the training sample L applies in the form

$$E_L[(\bar{f}(X;L) - E[Y|X])^2] = (E_L[\bar{f}(X;L) - E[Y|X]])^2 \\ +E_L[(\bar{f}(X;L) - E_L[\bar{f}(X;L)])^2], \tag{3.42}$$

where the first term on the right side of (3.42) is the square of the bias expectation, and the second term is the variance of the model $\bar{f}(X;D)$.

This theorem shows that, in terms of a random sampling L, the ensemble model error ε is represented as the sum of the square of the bias and the variance of the model itself. In this bias-variance tradeoff, an optimal solution should be sought empirically. Other theoretical results under the relevant assumptions are proved in [60, 61, 22].

3.4.2. Methods for Creating Ensembles

In ensemble learning, the base models are used as building blocks to generate secondary models by combining the results of several of them. It is known from many studies that the best ensemble model is obtained when the base models have low statistical indicators; therefore, they are also called "weak learners" [22, 54]. These weak models are such because they exhibit large deviations from modelled data or because they have too high variance and are not stable. Therefore, to construct an ensemble, one must first select the appropriate base models to be aggregated.

Combining base models in ensemble learning takes place in three main ways:

- Bagging. A uniform algorithm with perturbed samples is applied, which often creates homogeneous weak learners (base models). These learners are trained independently of each other in parallel, and their results are combined with voting in classification and some kind of linear averaging process in regression [62].
- Boosting. The same algorithm is used, and the learning is done sequentially in an adaptive way (the current model depends on the previous ones); it combines their results, following a certain strategy [54, 56].
- Stacking. An ensemble by stacking is created according to the stacking generalization paradigm [54, 56, 63]. Here, the base models are designed as strong learners, but as diverse as possible. In the second level, these models are retrained with a meta-algorithm different from them to extract a model with better properties than the base ones. It is also possible to meta-learn with several algorithms and stack the resulting second-level models, etc. Here, a well-known option is combining linear regressions (see [64]).

A huge number of publications in the field of ensemble learning are available in the literature. Comparative studies between different methods can be found in [22, 57, 65, 66].

We should note in particular that there is a great deal of confusion in the literature between the terms "ensemble" and "stacking." Many authors report ensembles in which models are created with diverse algorithms, and conversely, combinations of models with the same algorithm are described as stacked. We adhere to the definitions given in this chapter, according to the leading specialists in the field.

3.4.3. Random Forests (RF)

Among the ensemble tree-based methods, the most popular is Random Forests (RF) developed by Breiman in 2001 [67]. As stated in [22], "on many problems the performance of random forests is very similar to boosting, and they are simpler to train and tune. As a consequence, random forests are popular and are implemented in a variety of packages." The original open Fortran code of the RF algorithm created by Leo Breiman and Adele Cutler [68] is implemented in the SPM software we use [45].

RF is an ensemble of multiple base unpruned CART models, each built with an independent bootstrap sample. It does not depend on the type of data distribution, works with numerical and categorical data, is applicable to multi-class classification and regression, models high-dimensional tasks, and is easily parallelizable.

RF hyperparameters are: number of trees (*mtree*), minimum observations in parent and child nodes (*nmin*) (for regression, the default *nmin* is at least 5), number of predictors randomly selected from the total number of predictors (*mtry*) separately for each split at each node of each ensemble component tree, etc. Default *mtry* =3 suggested and studied in [67].

An RF model may be built from tens or hundreds of independent CART trees. It differs from standard bagging and boosting methods in a characteristic way of forming the test samples so as to obtain a large collection of different decorrelated trees. The source sample of original data is randomly divided into two parts, with one part containing about 1/3 of the data set aside for testing. This subsample is called Out-of-Bag (OOB). The remaining 2/3 of the data is used to construct bootstrap samples by random sampling with replacement, so that 100% of the size of the original data is obtained in each bootstrap sample. For each such sample, a tree is built according to the hyperparameters set at the input of the algorithm [69]. These trees are maximum (unpruned). The resulting model is validated on the OOB test sample. Complete information about the arithmetic mean statistics of the test model with OOB is displayed.

The final RF model is the arithmetic mean of the predictions of the single base *M=mtree* trees according to formula (3.39).

RF provides additional functions for determining variable importance and the relative variable importance of predictors in the generated model. RF method is highly efficient for prediction, multiclass classification, filling missing values, error visualization, and more.

3.4.4. Adaptively Resampling and Combine Algorithm (Arcing)

Arcing is a class of boosting algorithms, of which the most famous and one we implement is the Arc-x4 variant, developed and studied in [32, 70]. This method is similar to the AdaBoost algorithm proposed by Freund and Schapire [71, 72]. In many studies, Arcing is not inferior in performance to other boosting algorithms, while at the same time, it is simpler and faster in the implemented software versions. However, it should be noted that the power of this method has not yet been well studied, including in the field of environmental science. To fill this gap, we have chosen it in some of our case studies.

Arcing generates dozens of trees for different bootstrap samples of the same size as the original data. The algorithm successively builds the model trees so that each subsequent tree improves the performance of the previous ones. This is due to the special sampling, whereby observations that were misclassified (or with large regression errors) in the previous trees are indexed with new weights, expecting to improve the performance of the next tree. For this purpose, each observation is assigned a weight according to the expression

$$w_{t+1}(V_i) = \frac{1+m(V_i)^4}{\sum_i(1+m(V_i)^4)}, \tag{3.43}$$

where $m(V_i)$ is the number of misclassified observation values V_i from all the previous models $1,2,\dots,t$. The final model is the arithmetic mean of all trees in the ensemble, as given by the general formula (3.39). This averaging used to obtain the final ensemble predictions is among the main differences between Arcing and Adaboost.

Arcing hyperparameters include the number of trees in the ensemble, the type of validation (CV), the sizes of the smallest allowable parent and child nodes, the number of predictors randomly selected from all predictors to split each node, etc. Based on our experience, we argue that the latter of these hyperparameters does not significantly affect the model results.

It is well known that the Arcing method produces models with small variance and bias. The same is true for the bagging approach. But Arcing is considered to reduce test data prediction errors more than bagging [57, 70].

The scheme for constructing an Arcing model is presented in Figure 3.9.

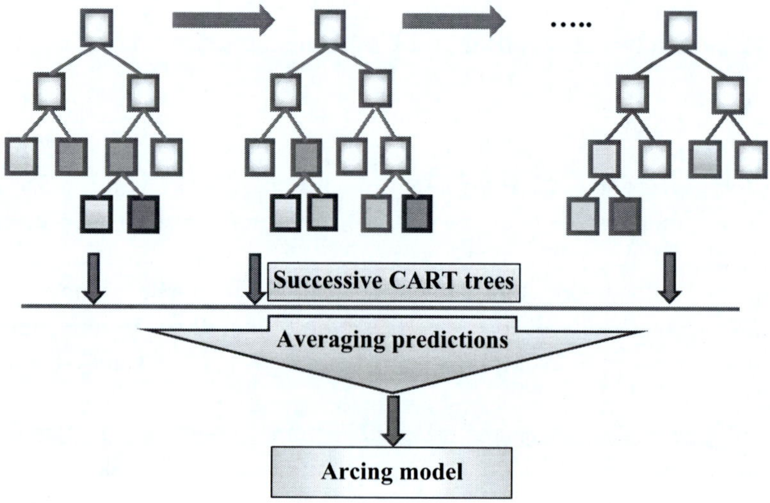

Figure 3.9. Building the Arcing model.

3.4.5. CART Ensembles and Bagging (EBag)

A typical but underexplored method for modeling in environmental science is CART Ensembles and Bagging (EBag). The EBag method was proposed by Leo Breiman in [62]. It is based on bootstrap aggregated samples. In the case of regression, different bootstrap samples of the same size are generated from the original training sample. With these samples, a set of tens of independent CART trees (single models) is constructed, and their predictions are averaged using (3.38) to obtain the final EBag model. We use the original Breiman algorithm implemented in the CART Ensembles and Bagger engine of Salford Predictive Modeler [45].

To build an EBag model, the following hyperparameters are set by the researcher: number of trees in the ensemble, minimum number of observations in parent and child nodes ($m1, m2, m2 \geq 5$), number of predictors that are randomly selected from all input predictors when splitting each node, type of validation, error loss function, etc. The main advantage of this method is the dramatic reduction of the error in the test samples and the reduction of their variance [62].

A peculiarity of the method is that the individual single trees of the ensemble exhibit significant differences in their predictive qualities, having individually low statistical indicators, i.e., in essence, they are weak learners. After aggregating them, the "weak" statistics are compensated, and the final ensemble model (classification or regression) has better performance [73].

Some heuristic methods have also been developed to detect the single patterns that worsen the general pattern and remove them using selective approaches [74-76].

The idea of the CART EBag building algorithm is illustrated in Figure 3.10.

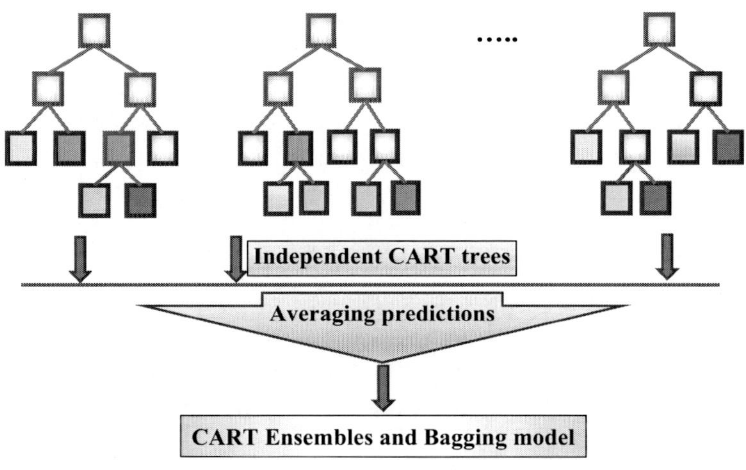

Figure 3.10. CART Ensembles and Bagging algorithm idea.

EBag provides additional functions for the relative mean and median values of variable importance in the model. It is suitable for a multiclass classification, handling missing values, statistics results of all individual trees in the ensemble, comparisons of statistics of all trees, various visualizations of results, etc.

3.5. Hybrid Methods

Hybrid methods are a sequence of applying two or more methods to solve a given problem. These methods can be classified into several groups, according to the use of the selected methods for data processing, analysis, and modeling, as follows:

- In the pre-processing data stage

Here, different approaches can be used to impute missing data – from linear interpolation to an ML algorithm, decomposition of a time series into parts using the usual seasonal decomposition, with wavelet transform, Fourier transform, or other methods, and the application of anomaly detection approaches, etc.

- In the data modeling stage

In this group, various methods can be applied for the identification, evaluation, and selection of the variables involved in the modeling, as well as for the optimization of the model parameters, mainly applying methods and approaches of mathematical optimization, statistical methods of comparison (regression, etc.).

When studying and forecasting time series, the data are usually complex, with outliers, trends, cycles, and often contain combinations of linear and non-linear patterns. With a hybrid approach, the linear and non-linear constituents can be modeled separately. This can be achieved using linear methods (such as ARIMA, multiple linear regression, etc.) or methods from some class of ML.

For example, in the classic work of Zhang G. P. [41], a hybrid model combining ARIMA and ANN was developed to leverage the capabilities of each method for linear and non-linear modeling, respectively. Combining is additive – the data is modeled with ARIMA, the linear part is extracted, and the residuals are modeled with neural networks. The sum of the predictions of the two models yields the final hybrid model.

- In the post-processing stage

When the goal is to improve the accuracy of prediction or classification as a result of modeling, or some other characteristic of the model, additional modeling of its residuals with an appropriate method is usually performed. This procedure can be repeated many times.

A more detailed overview of hybrid methods can be found in [67, pp. 747-748] and the sources cited therein.

3.5.1. Additive Hybrid Approach

Sometimes, in the case of time-series analysis, when diagnosing the residuals of a constructed model, the ACF or other characteristic shows unsatisfactory accuracy, unwanted serial correlation, and significant errors in the results. This requires further refinement and correction of the results of the obtained model, as written above in the post-processing stage. For this purpose, error modeling and residual dependency extraction can be applied. This can be done using the main method or another one suitable for the occasion. If necessary, some authors repeat the procedure iteratively to achieve an optimal result.

Since the error distribution is usually close to normal, in such cases, we will apply the ARIMA method. Thus, we obtain a hybrid ML-based-ARIMA error model with improved statistical performance and predictive accuracy. The same approach can be performed with other suitable methods.

Let the initial model $\hat{f}^{(1)}$ has an error $\varepsilon^{(1)}$ and the second model for predicting $\varepsilon^{(1)}$ has an error $\varepsilon^{(2)}$. Then, after an additive hybridization of the two models, we will get

$$Y = \hat{f}^{(1)} + \varepsilon^{(1)}, \quad \varepsilon^{(1)} = \hat{\varepsilon}^{(1)} + \varepsilon^{(2)} \;\rightarrow\; \hat{Y} = \hat{f}^{(1)} + \hat{\varepsilon}^{(1)}, \tag{3.44}$$

where the error of the hybrid model $\hat{Y}$ has an error equal to $\varepsilon^{(2)}$.

3.5.2. Stacking Paradigm in Machine Learning

Stacking can be viewed as a generalization of many diverse ensemble methods. On the other hand, it can be viewed as a specific combination method that combines by learning [56]. It needs to be noted that in this book, the concept of "stacking" assumes a combination of the results of various algorithms, unlike the concept of the "ensemble method," where one algorithm is applied to multiple subsets [77].

According to Wolpert's terminology [63], the original data and the models constructed from them in the first stage are referred to as level-0 data and level-0 models (or base learners), respectively. Then, the obtained set of cross-validated predictions and the second-stage learning algorithm are considered as level-1 data and the level-1 generalizer (or meta-learner), see [63, 64, 54]. The target variable is the same for the two levels. The stacking process can continue at higher levels as long as the performance of the resulting models increases.

A simplified outline of the stacking idea is shown in Figure 3.11.

In general, when implementing the stacking paradigm, it is recommended to observe several important factors that lead to better results:

- The number of base learners should be from 3 to 8 [54];
- The accuracy of base learners should be high, i.e., to be strong learners;
- To choose diverse base models;
- To select an appropriate meta-learner at the next level.

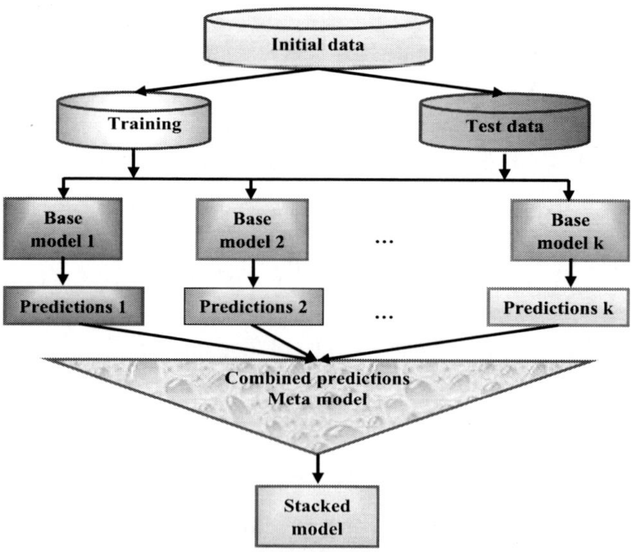

Figure 3.11. Main components and levels of the general stacking procedure.

Achieving diversity is a discussion issue, and not only because there is no generally accepted formal definition [78]. So far, there is no unified opinion or results that resolve this requirement in the general case. The problem comes from the fact that when the base learners are strong and their accuracy in classifying or predicting the original data is very high, they will be almost equal. In order to obtain a better stacked model from each of them, it is necessary that these models account for different specific patterns in the data.

To achieve diversity, the most essential thing is the application of as many different algorithms as possible, including ANN, deep learning, SVM, ensemble tree learning, etc. Moreover, these different algorithms should be applied with radically different initial samples, different types of learning strategies, different subsets of predictors, rotated samples (for example, with PCA or another method), diverse transformations of the data, hyperparameter optimization, and more, different for each learner [77].

The building of a stacked model, superior to all its constituents, depends significantly on the chosen meta-learner, which combines the predictions (see Figure 3.11). It should be different from the lower-level algorithms used. In addition, we will note that the application of multiple linear regression usually does not lead to good results, especially if the base learners are multicollinear. In the case of multicollinearity, a stacked model with slightly improved statistics was built using factor analysis in [79].

Also, there are no known good methods for assessing the degree of diversity. In the case of classifier ensembles, in [78], 10 types of statistical measures were studied, but the authors concluded that there are "some doubts about the usefulness of diversity measures in building classifier ensembles in real-life pattern recognition problems." From our experience, we should mention good results obtained by applying stacking for regression problems in [77], where most of the approaches described above in this subsection were used, and the MARS method was chosen as the meta-learner. For regression problems, the check for diversity between base models can be performed with non-parametric statistical tests for 2-related samples, such as the Wilcoxon signed rank test, the McNemar test, the Friedman test for k related samples, and others.

Modeling with model stacking is a challenging task that requires patience and experience on the part of the researcher.

3.6. Used Software in the Book

There are over 30 specialized mathematical and statistical software packages that can be used for time series analysis (see, for example, https://en.wikipedia.org/wiki/Comparison_of_statistical_packages).

The research and case studies in this book were conducted with the following statistical analysis packages:

- Salford Predictive Modeler (SPM), owned by Minitab [45];
- Wolfram Mathematica [80];
- IBM SPSS Statistics [31];
- EViews software for Windows [81] (demo version).

References

[1] Box, G. E. P., Jenkins, G. M., Reinsel, G. S., Ljung, G. M., 2016. *Time Series Analysis, Forecasting and Control, 5th edn.*, John Wiley & Sons. Inc, New Jersey.

[2] Mills, T. C., 2019. A*pplied Time Series Analysis: A Practical Guide to Modeling and Forecasting.* Academic Press.

[3] Pankratz, A., 1991. *Forecasting with Dynamic Regression Models*. John Wiley & Sons, New York.

[4] He, Y., Novac J. and Glosemeyer D., 2007. Mathematica Time Series: A Fully Integrated Environment for Time-Dependent Data Analysis. *Wolfram Research*, Inc., Illinois, USA. http://media.wolfram.com/documents/TimeSeries Documentation.pdf.

[5] Dickey, D. A. and Fuller, W. A., 1979. Distribution of the estimators for autoregressive time series with a unit root. *Journal of the American Statistical Association*, 74(366a), pp. 427-431.

[6] Nash, J. E. and Sutcliffe J. V., 1970. River flow forecasting through conceptual models: I. A discussion of principles. *Journal of Hydrology*, 10, pp. 282-290.

[7] Akaike, H., 1974. A new look at the statistical model identification. *IEEE Transactions on Automatic Control*, 19(6), 716-723.

[8] Schwarz, G., 1978. *Estimating the dimension of a model. Annals of Statistics*, 6, pp. 461-464.

[9] Burnham K. P. and Anderson D. R., 2002. *Model selection and inference: a practical information-theoretic approach.* 2nd edn. Springer, New York.

[10] Liddle A. R., 2008. *Information criteria for astrophysical model selection*. Cornell University Library.

[11] Christensen, R., 2011. *Plane Answers to Complex Questions: The Theory of Linear Models. 4nd edn.*, Springer.

[12] Mienye, I. D. and Sun, Y., 2022. A survey of ensemble learning: Concepts, algorithms, applications, and prospects. *IEEE Access*. 16(10), pp. 99129-99149.

[13] Aihounton, G. B. and Henningsen, A., 2021. Units of measurement and the inverse hyperbolic sine transformation. The *Econometrics Journal*, 24(2), pp. 334-35.

[14] Mallat, S. G., 1989. A theory for multiresolution signal decomposition: The wavelet representation, *IEEE Transactions on Pattern Analysis and Machine Intelligence*, 11(7), pp. 674-693.

[15] Daubechies, I., 1988. Orthonormal bases of compactly supported wavelets. *Communications on Pure and Applied Mathematics*, 41(7), pp. 909-996.

[16] Burrus, T. V., Burrus, C., Narasimhan, K., Guo, Y. and Li, C., 1998. *Introduction to Wavelets and Wavelet Transforms: A Primer*, Prentice Hall, New Jersey.

[17] Percival, D. B. and Walden, A. T., 2000. *Wavelet methods for time series analysis.* Cambridge University Press.

[18] Schlüter, S. and Deuschle, C., 2010. Using wavelets for time series forecasting: Does it pay off? *IWQW Discussion Papers, 4*. Friedrich-Alexander University Erlangen-Nuremberg, Institute for Economics (IWQW).

[19] Osowski, S. and Garanty, K., 2007. Forecasting of the daily meteorological pollution using wavelets and support vector machine. *Engineering Applications of Artificial Intelligence*, 20(6), pp. 745-755.

[20] Donoho, D. L. and Johnstone, I. M., 1994. Ideal spatial adaptation by wavelet shrinkage. *Biometrika*, 81(3), pp. 425-455.

[21] Donoho, D. L., 1995. De-noising by soft-thresholding. *IEEE Transactions on Information Theory*, 41(3), pp. 613-627.

[22] Hastie, T., Tibshirani, R., Friedman, J., 2009. *The Elements of Statistical Learning: Data Mining, Inference, and Prediction.* Springer.

[23] Nason, G. P., 1996. Wavelet shrinkage using cross-validation. *Journal of the Royal Statistical Society: Series B (Methodological)*, 58(2), pp. 463-479.

[24] Guo, T., Zhang, T., Lim, E., Lopez-Benitez, M., Ma, F. and Yu, L., 2022. A review of wavelet analysis and its applications: Challenges and opportunities. *IEEe Access,* 10, pp. 58869-58903.

[25] Grané, A. and Veiga, H., 2010. Wavelet-based detection of outliers in financial time series. *Computational Statistics and Data Analysis*, 54(11), pp. 2580-2593.

[26] Halidou, A., Mohamadou, Y., Ari, A. A. A. and Zacko, E. J. G., 2023. Review of wavelet denoising algorithms. *Multimedia Tools and Applications*, 82(27), pp. 41539-41569.

[27] Granger, C. W., 1969. Investigating causal relations by econometric models and cross-spectral methods. *Econometrica: Journal of the Econometric Society*, 37(3), pp. 424-438.

[28] Gujarati, D. N., 2004. *Basic Econometrics* (Ch. 10), 4th ed., McGraw–Hill.

[29] Koop, G., 2000. *Analysis of Economic Data*. John Wiley & Sons, New York.

[30] Diks, C. and Panchenko, V., 2006. A new statistic and practical guidelines for nonparametric Granger causality testing. *Journal of Economic Dynamics and Control*, 30(9-10), pp. 1647-1669.

[31] IBM SPSS Statistics, https://www.ibm.com/products/spss-statistics.

[32] Breiman, L., 1996. Bias, variance, and arcing classifiers, *Technical Report 460,* Statistics Department, University of California, https://www.stat.berkeley.edu/ users/breiman/arcall96.pdf.

[33] Breiman, L., 1996. Heuristics of instability and stabilization in model selection. *The annals of statistics*, 24(6), pp. 2350-2383.

[34] Craven, P. and Wahba, G., 1979. Smoothing noisy data with spline functions: estimating the correct degree of smoothing by the method of generalized cross-validation. *Numerische Mathematik*, 31(4), S. 377-403.

[35] Izenman J., 2008. Modern Multivariate Statistical Techniques. *Regression, Classification, and Manifold Learning.* Springer, New York.

[36] Breiman, L., Friedman, J. H., Stone, C. J. and Olshen, R. A., 1984. *Classification and Regression Trees.* Chapman & Hall Wadsworth, Inc., New York.

[37] Quinlan, J. R., 1986. Induction of decision trees. *Machine learning*, 1, pp. 81-106.

[38] Steinberg, D. and Golovnya, M., 2007. CART 6.0 User's Guide. *Salford Systems*, San Diego, CA.

[39] Deng, H., Runger, G. and Tuv, E., 2011. Bias of importance measures for multi-valued attributes and solutions. In *Artificial Neural Networks and Machine Learning–ICANN 2011: 21st International Conference on Artificial Neural Networks*, Espoo, Finland, June 14-17, 2011, *Proceedings, Part II 21* (pp. 293-300). Springer Berlin Heidelberg.

[40] Gocheva-Ilieva, S., Voynikova, D., Stoimenova, M., Ivanov, A. and Iliev, I., 2019. Regression trees modeling of time series for air pollution analysis and forecasting. *Neural Computing and Applications*, 31(12), pp. 9023-9039.

[41] Zhang, G. P., 2003. Time series forecasting using a hybrid ARIMA and neural network model. *Neurocomputing*, 50, pp. 159-175.

[42] Ljung, G. and Box, G., 1978. On a measure of lack of fit in time series models. *Biometrika*, 65, pp. 297-303.

[43] De Gooijer, J. G. and Kumar, K., 1992. Some recent developments in non-linear time series modelling, testing, and forecasting. *International Journal of Forecasting*, 8, pp. 135-156.

[44] Friedman, J. H., 1991. Multivariate adaptive regression splines (with discussion). *Annals of Statistics*, 19(1), pp. 1-141.

[45] Salford Predictive Modeler (SPM). https://www.minitab.com/en-us/products/spm/.

[46] Steinberg D., Bernstein B., Colla P. and Martin K., 2001. *MARS User Guide, Salford Systems*, San Diego, CA.

[47] Gocheva-Ilieva, S., 2016. *Analytical, Statistical and Intelligent Modeling Methods.* Dissertation of Doctor of Science, Plovdiv University Paisii Hilendarski. (in Bulgarian).

[48] Kelleher J. D., McNamee B. and D'Arcy A., 2015. *Fundamentals of Machine Learning for Predictive Data Analytics: Algorithms, Worked Examples, and Case Studies.* The MIT Press.

[49] Howe J., 2006. The rise of crowdsourcing. *Wired Magazine*, 14 (6), pp. 1-4.

[50] Zhou, Z. H., Wu, J. and Tang, W., 2002. Ensembling neural networks: many could be better than all. *Artificial intelligence*, 137(1-2), pp. 239-263.

[51] Džeroski, S. and Ženko, B., 2004. Is combining classifiers with stacking better than selecting the best one? *Machine Learning*, 54(3), pp. 255–273.

[52] Bates, J. M. and Granger, C. W., 1969. The combination of forecasts. Journal of the Operational Research Society, 20(4), pp. 451-468.

[53] Newbold, P. and Granger, C. W., 1974. Experience with forecasting univariate time series and the combination of forecasts. *Journal of the Royal Statistical Society: Series A (General)*, 137(2), pp. 131-146.

[54] Kuncheva, L. I., 2004. *Combining Pattern Classifiers: Methods and Algorithms*. John Wiley and Sons, Inc., Hoboken.

[55] Sollich, P. and Krogh, A., 1995. Learning with ensembles: How overfitting can be useful, *Advances in Neural Information Processing Systems*, 8, pp. 190-196.

[56] Zhou, Z. H., 2012. *Ensemble Methods: Foundations and Algorithms*. CRC Press, Boca Raton.

[57] Bauer, E. and Kohavi, R., 1999. An empirical comparison of voting classification algorithms: Bagging, boosting, and variants. *Machine Learning*, 36, pp. 105-139.

[58] Efron, B. and Tibshirani, R. J., 1994. *An introduction to the bootstrap*. Chapman and Hall/CRC.

[59] Geman, S., Bienenstock, E. and Doursat R., 1992. Neural networks and the bias/variance dilemma. *Neural computation*, 4(1), pp. 1-58.

[60] Krogh, A. and Sollich, P., 1997. Statistical mechanics of ensemble learning. *Physical Review E - Statistical Physics, Plasmas, Fluids, and Related Interdisciplinary Topics*, 55(1), pp. 811-825.

[61] Ueda, N. and Nakano, R., 1996, June. Generalization error of ensemble estimators. In *Proceedings of International Conference on Neural Networks* (ICNN'96) (Vol. 1, pp. 90-95). IEEE.

[62] Breiman, L., 1996. Bagging predictors. *Machine Learning*, 24(2), pp. 123-140.

[63] Wolpert, D., 1992. Stacked generalization. *Neural Networks*, 5, pp. 241-259.

[64] Breiman, L., 1996. Stacked regressions. *Machine Learning*, 24, pp. 49-64.

[65] Opitz, D. and Maclin, R., 1999. Popular ensemble methods: An empirical study. *Journal of Artificial Intelligence Research*, 11, pp. 169-198.

[66] Petropoulos, F., Apiletti, D., Assimakopoulos, V., Babai. M. Z., Barrow, D. K., Taieb, S. B. et al., 2022. Forecasting: theory and practice. *International Journal of Forecasting*, 38(3), pp. 705-871.

[67] Breiman, L., 2001. Random forests. *Machine Learning*, 45(1), pp. 5-32.

[68] Breiman, L and Cutler, A. 2004. *Random Forests Fortran code.* https://www.stat.berkeley.edu/~breiman/RandomForests/cc_software.htm.

[69] Cutler, A., Cutler, D. R. and Stevens, J. R., 2012. Random forests. In *Ensemble Machine Learning: Methods and Applications* (pp. 157-175).

[70] Breiman, L., 1998. Arcing classifiers. *The Annals of Statistics*, 26(3), pp. 801-849.

[71] Freund, Y. and Schapire, R. E., 1997. A decision-theoretic generalization of on-line learning and an application to boosting. *Journal of Computer and System Sciences*, 55(1), pp. 119-139.

[72] Freund, Y. and Schapire, R. E., 1996, July. Experiments with a new boosting algorithm. In *icml* (Vol. 96, pp. 148-156).

[73] Steinberg D. and Golovnya, M., 2014. *Tree ensembles and extensions: An overview of treeNet, random forests, ISLE model compression & RuleLearner.* http://info.salford-systems.com/jsm-2013-ctw2 2014.

[74] Wei, L., Wan, S., Guo, J. and Wong, K. K., 2017. A novel hierarchical selective ensemble classifier with bioinformatics application. *Artificial intelligence in medicine*, 83, pp. 82-90.

[75] Zhou, Z. H. and Tang, W., 2003. Selective ensemble of decision trees. In Rough Sets, Fuzzy Sets, Data Mining, and Granular Computing: *9th International Conference, RSFDGrC 2003*, Chongqing, China, May 26–29, 2003 Proceedings 9 (pp. 476-483). Springer Berlin Heidelberg.

[76] Gocheva-Ilieva, S., Yordanova, A. and Kulina, H., 2022. Predicting the 305-day milk yield of Holstein-Friesian cows depending on the conformation traits and farm using simplified selective ensembles. *Mathematics*, 10(8), art. 1254.

[77] Gocheva-Ilieva, S. G., Ivanov, A. V. and Stoimenova-Minova, M. P., 2022. Prediction of daily mean PM10 concentrations using random forest and CART ensemble and bagging stacked by MARS. *Sustainability*, 14(2), art. 798.

[78] Kuncheva, L. I. and Whitaker, C. J., 2003. Measures of diversity in classifier ensembles and their relationship with the ensemble accuracy. *Machine learning*, 51, pp. 181-207.

[79] Gocheva-Ilieva, S., Kulina, H. and Yordanova, A., 2022, November. Stacking machine learning models using factor analysis to predict the output laser power. In *2022 International Conference on Electrical, Computer, Communications and Mechatronics Engineering (ICECCME)* (pp. 1-6). IEEE.

[80] Wolfram Mathematica, https://www.wolfram.com/mathematica/.

[81] EViews software, https://www.eviews.com/home.html.

Chapter 4

Forecasting PM_{10} Using ARIMA and CART with Variable Sample Size

Abstract

This chapter applies and compares particulate matter (PM_{10}) concentration models built with the ARIMA and CART methods. Especially, the effect of sample size on the performance of the models was also investigated. A CART model with a sample size of 760 cases was shown to outperform models with four times larger samples. Previous, but weaker, results for CART models on the same studied data were obtained in our published work [1].

Keywords: autoregression, bagging, boosting, cross-validation, dataset reduction, machine learning, particulate matter

4.1. Introduction

One of the more harmful air pollutants all around the world is particulate matter PM_{10}, with a diameter equal to or less than 10 microns. Modelling PM_{10} data has been the focus of extensive research. Prediction of the concentrations of this pollutant is done with a variety of statistical and ML approaches. Some of these results are included in the literature review in section 1.3. To obtain forecasts of future PM_{10} values, regression-type models are constructed. It is well known that PM_{10} levels depend on complex interactions among many parameters and are the result of a combination of regional background, urban and traffic concentrations [2], atmospheric and meteorological conditions [3], temporal variables, and more. Also, in addition to these potential predictors in PM_{10} models, the inclusion of lagged PM_{10} via a feature extraction technique is considered to improve model performance [3, 4]. For example, Stadlober et al. [3] showed that lagged PM_{10} is a more important variable than temporal or meteorological variables in the forecasting of PM_{10} in urban areas.

In general, it is considered that PM_{10} prediction in urban areas is more difficult than the prediction of other air pollutants (e.g., NO_2) [5].

In recent years in Bulgaria, it has been announced that an average of 66-68% of mortality is related to this problematic pollutant. Even in some small and mountainous villages, high levels of PM_{10} are observed. This chapter explores such a case. Assuming that local conditions (site geography, manufacturing plants, household processes, etc.) are relatively invariable or have constant features, we will mainly investigate the influence of meteorological and atmospheric influences on PM_{10} concentrations. For this purpose, classical ARIMA and Classification and Regression Tree (CART) methods to analyze the data are applied and compared.

In particular, we will also consider the optimization of the sample size and the influence of this effect on the performance of the built models. In the literature, the problem of choosing the optimal sample size has been well studied in classical statistical methods (see, for instance, [6]). In modern data mining, similar methods have not yet been thoroughly studied. This relates in particular to the impact of sample size on the performance of the CART method.

We will empirically show that by reducing the sample size to a certain limit, the prediction of the models improves. On the other hand, determining an optimal smaller sample size automatically leads to a reduction in the required computer resources (time and memory) to perform the modelling.

Under real-world conditions and applying the prediction approach with little data change, the smaller size allows for distributed computing in networks and is suitable for use with mobile devices and parallel architectures. This aspect is essential for the developed predictive approach, as part of the objectives of the EMULSION project [7].

The quantitative results for the performance of the built models are as follows: ARIMA reaches $R^2 = 82\%$ agreement with the measured data, and CART reaches 87%. Diagnostics of the residuals of the models were made. These were applied to forecast PM_{10} levels 3 days ahead.

The analyses are performed using IBM SPSS Statistics and the CART engine of Salford Predictive Modeler (SPM) [8, 9]. Each model in SPM software is calculated within 1-2 seconds on a standard Windows PC.

4.2. Study Area and Data

In this section, the study area and a detailed description of the -data used are presented.

- Study area

The area selected for research is the town of Smolyan, a small regional town in southern Bulgaria, located in the central part of the Rhodope Mountains. Smolyan is the smallest regional town in Bulgaria, its population is around 30,000 people according to the 2024 census. The city is 25 km long, making it one of the longest towns in Bulgaria. The geographical location of Smolyan determines the predominance of eastern winds. The climate in the town is transitional-continental with a pronounced influence from the White Sea, located less than 100 kilometers to the south. The higher parts of the district are characterized by a mountainous climate, cool and humid summers, mild winters, and warm, long autumns.

The retention of the snow cover is in the range of 80 to 120 days. Smolyan is located at 1035 meters above sea level. The average annual rainfall that falls in the town is between 700 and 900 liters. The minimum average monthly temperature is 5.2°C, and the maximum average monthly temperature is 22.7°C. Several enterprises are located on the territory of the town, which are mainly in the processing industry sector. Various metalworking machines, wires, cables, plastic components for the electronics, food, and automotive industries are produced, as well as mechanical processing of metals, casting of cast iron, aluminum, and others.

- Data description

In this chapter, real data on PM_{10} concentrations are studied, as well as weather and atmospheric conditions on an average diurnal scale in the town of Smolyan. The data are for the period from 01.01.2010 to 30.04.2018. The target variable in the modeling is designated as *Pm*10. For the statistical analysis, the influence of the following variables was taken into account: minimum air temperature - *minTemp* (°C), maximum air temperature - *maxTemp* (°C), precipitation - *prec* (%), air pressure - *AP* (mb), relative humidity - *RH* (%), cloud cover - *CC* (%), wind speed - *WS* (m/s), wind direction - *WD* (categorical), weather - *whtr* (categorical). In addition, there are also used the lagged variable of $Pm10$ for the previous day: $Pm10$<1>, $(\mu g/m^3)$ and lagged variables for one and two previous days of the minimum and maximum average daily temperatures – *minTemp*<1> (°C), *minTemp*<2> (°C), *maxTemp*<1> (°C), *maxTemp*<2> (°C). Two predictor variables of numerical type were also added to account for the time – *month_* and *month_day*. These variables take values as follows

$$month\_ = \{1,2,\ldots,12\},$$
$$month\_day = month\_ + \frac{day\_-0.5}{md}, \tag{4.1}$$

where $day\_ = \{1,2,\ldots,27,\ldots,md\}$ and md is equal to the number of days in a month.

Descriptive statistics were applied to the original data used for the analyses. The results are presented in Table 4.1.

The sample size of the source data for the specified period is N= 3040. Of them, for PM_{10}, 115 are missing, or that's 3.77% of the total. In subsequent analyses, linear interpolation was applied to fill in missing data. The last 3 cases from the samples are used for prediction.

Table 4.1. Descriptive statistics of the initial numerical data for Smolyan, Bulgaria

Statistics	$Pm10$ $\mu g/m^3$	*minTemp*, °C	*maxTemp*, °C	*WS*, m/s	*prec*, %	*RH*, %	*AP*, mbar	*CC*, %
N	2922	3037	3037	3037	3037	3037	3037	3037
N missing	115	0	0	0	0	0	0	0
Mean	45.12	8.56	13.96	6.88	4.36	0.766	1016	0.334
Median	34.12	9.00	14.00	6.00	0.80	0.77	1016	0.26
Std. Dev.	29.82	9.88	9.06	3.19	8.16	0.13	6.93	0.27
Skewness	1.82	-0.21	-0.22	1.49	4.33	-0.25	0.22	0.80
Std. Error Skewness	0.045	0.044	0.044	0.044	0.044	0.044	0.044	0.044
Kurtosis	4.13	-0.62	-0.80	3.78	33.92	-0.71	0.34	-0.33
Std. Err. Kurtosis	0.091	0.089	0.089	0.089	0.089	0.089	0.089	0.089
Minimum	9.14	-23	-15	1.0	0	0.28	990	0
Maximum	260	29	33	28	126.1	1.0	1039	1

From the statistics in Table 4.1, it is clear that for the studied period, the average value of the PM_{10} pollutant was $45.15\mu g/m^3$. During the considered period, the maximum concentration of PM_{10} of $260\,\mu g/m^3$ was reached, which means that the value is 5 times higher than the maximum permissible national and European average daily norm of 50 $\mu g/m^3$ [10]. These results also demonstrate that the average concentration of PM_{10} exceeds the maximum permissible threshold of 20 $\mu g/m^3$ prescribed by the World Health Organization.

Figure 4.1 (a) illustrates the sequence plot of the initial measured values of the air pollutant PM_{10} in the town of Smolyan for the studied period. The horizontal dashed line at the level of 50 $\mu g/m^3$ reflects the maximum permissible European threshold for safe health. A large number of PM_{10} exceeding values over this limit are observed. It can also be noted from the sequence plot that the excesses occur mainly during the cold winter months. The geographical position of the town, some of the weather conditions, for example, the weak wind, favor the retention of atmospheric pollutants.

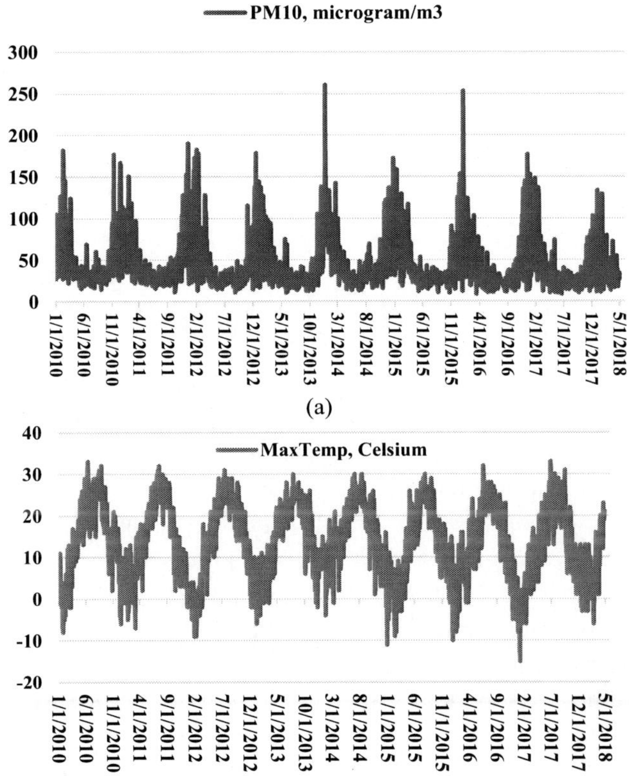

(b)

Figure 4.1. (a) Actual PM_{10} daily concentrations in the town of Smolyan. The horizontal dashed line shows the prescribed EU and national daily limit of 50 $\mu g/m^3$; (b) Maximum average daily temperature compared to PM_{10}.

Other major problems for poor air quality in the town identified in the regional reports are the sources of fine dust due to domestic heating, transport, and industry. These are the main reasons for the great number of high concentrations and exceedances in winter.

In this chapter, two methods, ARIMA [11, 12] and CART [13, 14], are applied to model the above-described data for the town of Smolyan. The aim is to establish the influence of meteorological factors that further contribute to high concentrations of PM_{10} in addition to the already mentioned causes, such as industry, domestic heating, and others. Appropriate mathematical models are sought to describe the data to the highest degree and to be applied to short-term predictions of future pollution. The best models are selected on the basis of the smallest relative error in the deviation of the model from the data of the dependent variable and reaching the largest value of the coefficient of determination R^2, i.e., approximation of the model to the highest degree to the real data.

4.3. The Application of ARIMA for PM_{10} Modeling

First, we will apply the classic stochastic ARIMA method, described in Chapter 3, paragraph 3.2. The application of the ARIMA method assumes that the data follow a normal or close to normal distribution. For our data, the distribution does not meet this requirement, as can be seen from the box-plot in Figure 4.2 (a). For this purpose, the Yeo-Jonson formula (2.10) [15] was applied to the dependent variable $Pm10$ and the best result was obtained for $\lambda = -0.3$. The transformed variable is denoted by $tPm10\_\_03$. Its distribution is close to normal, as shown in Figure 4.2 (b).

Next, the newly transformed variable $tPm10\_\_03$ was used to perform the analyses for the ARIMA models. Its sequence plot is shown in Figure 4.3. A weak downward linear trend is observed in this figure.

When building parametric ARIMA models, we look for models of $tPm10\_\_03$ of the form ARIMA(p, d, q). We will first check whether the series should be assumed to be stationary or not. For this purpose, we use the Dickey-Fuller and Phillips-Perron unit root tests, calculated using Wolfram Mathematica [16, 17]. The results are given in Table 4.2. Since all four p-values are greater than 0.05, we conclude that there is a trend. With a trend check of the differentiated order, it turned out that the sought trend is of the first order. This way, we established the trend parameter d = 1.

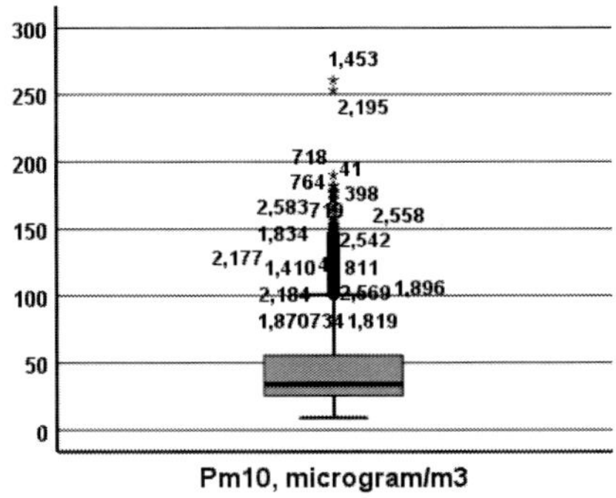

(a)

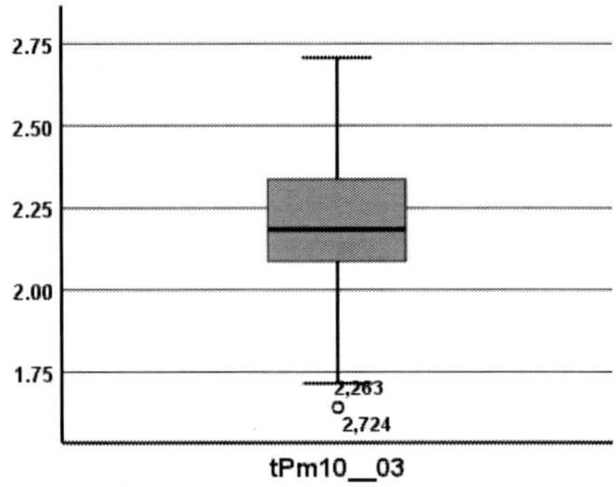

(b)

Figure 4.2. Box-plots of the distributions: (a) for the initial time series *Pm*10; (b) for the transformed time series *tPm*10__03.

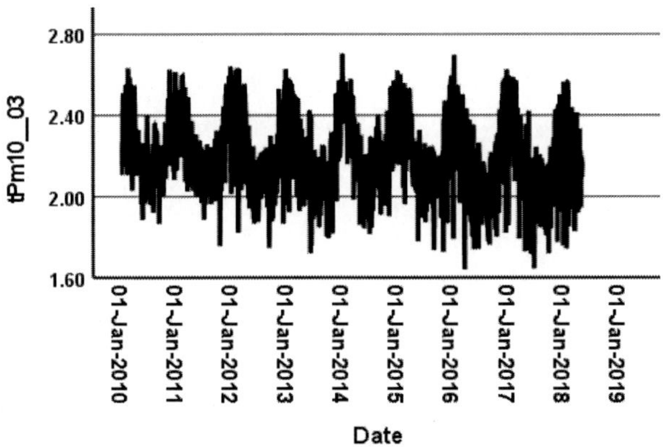

Figure 4.3. Sequence plot of the transformed time series *tPm*10__03.

Table 4.2. Unit root test results for time series tPm10__03

Statistical Test	Statistic	Significance (p-value)
Dickey-Fuller F	-4.86760	0.12921
Dickey-Fuller T	-1.56748	0.11005
Phillips-Perron F	-1.21587	0.43866
Phillips-Perron T	-0.79493	0.37168

To determine p and q, we examine the sequence plots of the autocorrelation functions (ACF) and partial ACF (PACF). For transformed time series, these functions are shown in Figure 4.4. From Figure 4.4, it can be seen that the ACF decreases slowly and almost monotonically, which means that there is no presence of short-term periodic or seasonal changes in the studied variable.

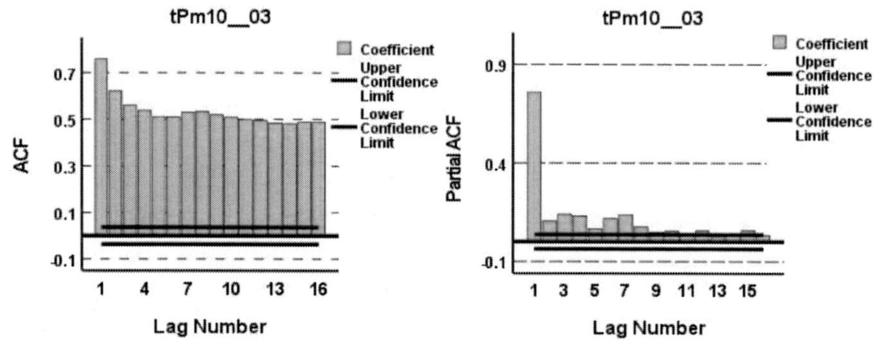

(a) (b)

Figure 4.4. ACF and PACF of transformed time series *tPm*10__03 for Smolyan.

The PACF plot demonstrates several outliers in the first lags, which allows determining possible values for the two parameters p and q. The PACF shows sharp jumps in lags 1, 3, and 7. This indicates that the *PM*10 model can be searched for autoregression and moving averages with up to 7 terms, i.e., the values of p and q are in the range $1 < p < 7$ and $1 < q < 7$.

- Construction and analysis of variable sample size ARIMA models

To determine the most appropriate ARIMA model, multiple models with different numbers of observations were built. Dependent variable is the transformed time series *tPm*10__03. Only predictors with numerical values can be used for ARIMA. In our task, the seven variables from Table 4.1 are: *minTemp, maxTemp, WS, prec, AP,* and *CC*. Models are evaluated using the statistical measures R^2, RMSE, and MAPE. Two tests for the autocorrelation of the residuals are applied: the Durbin-Watson, in which the ideal case for non-serial correlation is 2, and the Ljung-Box portfolio. The resulting models with the best parameters are presented in Table 4.3.

First, the univariate model *A*1 of the form ARIMA(1,0,7) was built using all data without predictors. From Table 4.3, it can be seen that the value of R^2 is 0.593, indicating that model *A*1 describes the data variation with up to 59%. The autoregressive component p=1, i.e., the level of pollution is most strongly influenced by the values of fine dust measured from the previous day. The component of the moving averages q=7, indicates that the stochastic changes are dependent on 7 previous terms within the time series.

The second model, *A*2, is of the form ARIMA/TR(0,1,3). It is built with the inclusion of predictors. Among them, significant in the model are the variables *maxTemp, WS, RH, prec*, and *AP*, with which it achieves better results. The coefficient of determination is 0.657, or the model *A*2 describes the data with up to 66%. The constructed models were tested for adequacy using the Ljung-Box residual autocorrelation statistic, where Sig. (i.e., p-value) is insignificant. This is the requirement for the lack of serial correlation in model residuals. However, the Durbin-Watson test for serial correlation with a value of 1.630 is not satisfactory enough, which may be due to unaccounted-for influences from other variables and factors.

Table 4.3. The best ARIMA models of *Pm*10 for Smolyan[a]

Model	Sample size	ARIMA	Predictors	Ljung-Box Sig.	R^2	RMSE, $\mu g/m^3$	MAPE	Durbin-Watson
*A*1	3040	ARIMA (0,1,7)	-	0.677	0.593	19.252	27.306	1.640
*A*2	3040	ARIMA/ TR (0,1,3)	*minTemp, maxTemp, AP, WS*	0.589	0.657	17.540	24.152	1.630
*A*3	1520	ARIMA/ TR (1,1,1)	*minTemp, maxTemp, AP, WS, RH*	0.584	0.667	16.781	25.841	1.577
*A*4	760	ARIMA/ TR (1,0,3)	*maxTemp, AP, WS*	0.491	0.623	17.486	28.113	1.515

[a] Statistics are computed after retransforming of the models.

- ARIMA with reduced number of observations

We also examine the effect of sample size on model performance. As a second option, from the initial number of cases *N*=3040, we take half of the more recent data, i.e., *N*1=1520. We denote the corresponding target variable by *tPm*10__03_1520. For this reduced sample, the first-order trend is preserved, as is the near-normal distribution of the dependent variable *tPm*10__03_1520. We repeat the procedures to build an adequate ARIMA model.

Table 4.4. Parameters of the ARIMA model *A*3 for Smolyan data

Variable	Component	Lag	Estimate	t	Sig.
*tPm*10__03_1520	AR	Lag 1	0.420	14.915	0.000
	Difference		1		
	MA	Lag 1	0.935	81.655	0.000
maxTemp	Numerator	Lag 0	0.014	9.812	0.000
		Lag 1	0.012	8.879	0.000
minTemp	Numerator	Lag 0	-0.005	-3.655	0.000
		Lag 1	-0.004	-2.087	0.037
		Lag 3	0.003	1.979	0.048
		Lag 4	-0.004	-4.089	0.000
WS	Numerator	Lag 0	-0.001	-2.070	0.039
RH	Delay		1		
	Numerator	Lag 0	-0.119	-3.149	0.002
		Lag 1	-0.118	-3.143	0.002
AP	Delay		1		
	Numerator	Lag 0	0.003	4.696	0.000
		Lag 1	0.003	4.698	0.000

The best model obtained using the seven predictors is of the form *A*3= ARIMA/TR(1,1,1). Its statistics are given in Table 4.3. The obtained values of R^2=0.667, as well as other statistics, are slightly better than those of model *A*2. In this case, halving the sample size did not significantly improve the quality of the ARIMA models.

Table 4.4 shows the parameters of the *A*3 model with their estimates. All parameters are significant at the 0.05 level.

Figure 4.5 shows the ACF and PACF of the residuals of model *A*3. The errors are negligibly small at the 95% confidence interval, allowing us to assume that the model is adequate, with no autocorrelations.

Similarly, a variant with a sample size of the most recent quarter of the initial data, $N2 = 760$ cases, was constructed. For this reduced sample, there is no longer a *Pm*10 trend, nor for the transformed variable labelled *tPm*10__03_760. The distribution is close to normal. The built model has the form ARIMA/TR(1,0,3) and is denoted by *A*4. Its corresponding statistics are shown in the last row of Table 4.4. It can be seen that they are unfavorable to the *A*3 model's statistics.

As a final result, we define the ARIMA model *A*3 with half of the initial data as the best one from the ARIMA series.

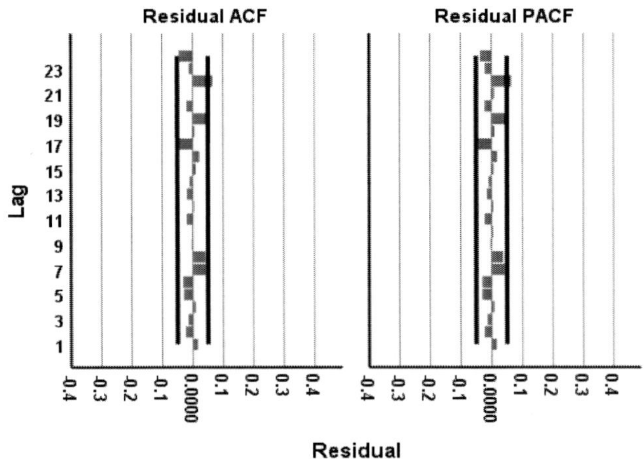

Figure 4.5. ACF and PACF of the residuals of ARIMA model *A*3 for Smolyan data.

4.4. CART Models with Variable Sample Size

The main idea of the present study is to gradually reduce the number of observations and determine whether the sample size affects the degree of approximation of the ML models to the actual data and the accuracy of the prediction results for future pollution. In this paragraph, CART regression models are built from the same data as in paragraph 4.2 and used in [1]. The CART method was described in detail in Chapter 3, paragraph 3.3.

In the subsequent statistical analyses, the data were not transformed, as transformations do not significantly affect ML algorithms, including CART. The dependent variable is denoted by *Pm*10.

The aim is to determine the influence of meteorological factors on PM_{10} levels in the town of Smolyan. Machine learning with V-fold cross-validation is applied in building the CART models, where the sample is split into a training and a test sample, which are two non-intersecting subsets. With V=10, the sample is randomly divided into 10 nearly equal subgroups. For each subgroup, the remaining 9 are used as a training sample, with which a CART tree is built. With the help of the obtained model, the values of the separated test 10% sample are predicted (see also Chapter 3, paragraph 3.3 and Figure 3.6).

To build the CART models, all 16 variables described in section 4.2, including numerical, categorical, and lagged variables, as well as two time-related variables, were used as predictors. Additional data for the last 3 days in the samples from 28 to 30 April 2018 are retained as holdout data for forecasting purposes.

After performing some preliminary experiments, it was determined that the resulting best models have the following hyperparameters: a minimum number of instances in a parent and child node m_1=10 and m_2=5, respectively. We consider the best model to be the one that achieves the smallest error statistic RMSE of the dependent variable and the highest value of the coefficient of determination R^2.

In our previous work [1], using CART, three optimal models of the dependent time series *Pm*10 were selected, denoted by *M*1, *M*2, and *M*3. Their statistics are given in the first three rows of Table 4.5 for comparison.

In this study, CART models are refined by using more terminal nodes in the trees, which are valid within one standard error (1-SE). This approach is used to avoid possible instability of the best reduced tree. In this case, from all the generated CART trees, the smallest one T_{**} is selected for which the mean square error (MSE) does not exceed the minimum $\hat{R}(T_*)$ with the addition of 1-SE according to the formula [18, 19].

$$\hat{R}(T_{**}) \leq \hat{R}(T_*) + SE\left(\hat{R}(T_*)\right), \tag{4.2}$$

where T_* is the tree with the minimal error.

Table 4.5. The best CART models of *Pm*10 for Smolyan with variable sample size

Model	Sample size	(m1, m2)	V-fold cross-validation	Number of the terminal nodes	R^2 Learn	RMSE, $\mu g/m^3$
*M*1	3037	(10,5)	10	20	0.674	16.941
*M*2	1518	(10,5)	10	31	0.790	13.187
*M*3	757	(10,5)	10	57	0.868	10.117
*M*4	3037	(10,5)	10	43	0.730	15.472
*M*5	1518	(10,5)	10	50	0.810	12.713
*M*6	757	(10,5)	10	60	0.870	10.181

The *M*4 model is built with 3037 data for the period from January 1, 2010, to April 27, 2018. The model's approximation to the real data is about 73%, which gives an improvement of more than 5% over the reference model *M*1 with the same sample size. The construction of the *M*5 model is similar, with the data halved by removing older measurements. This means that the sample contains N=1518 data, and the studied period is from February 28, 2014, to April 27, 2018.

The resulting model *M5* has better performance than model *M2*, which was obtained by analyzing the same data in [1]. *M5* describes the data with up to 81% accuracy. The latest newly built model *M6* was similarly with a reduced dataset of size N=757, so that the data included in the analysis are for the period from 29 March 2016 to 27 April 2018. This model is the best one for which the specified sample size is entirely suitable for performing a sufficiently accurate analysis of the values of the air pollutant PM_{10}.

Among the selected models presented in Table 4.5, the new refined model *M6* obtained with the smallest data sample stands out as the best according to the obtained statistical indicators. Its approximation to the actual data is R^2=87% with RMSE=10.181 $\mu g/m^3$. This is most likely due to the greater impact of more recent observations on model quality.

- Analysis of the CART models for Smolyan

The CART method makes it possible to determine the percentage influence of the predictors included in the models. Table 4.6 presents the results of the influence of the predictors in the constructed CART models from Table 4.5. The most significant predictor across all models, with a score of 100, having the greatest influence on the *Pm*10 is the level of particulate matter measured the previous day. This is interpreted as permanent retention of particles in the air for more than 24 hours. Table 4.6 shows that the second most influential predictor obtained for all models is the minimum average daily temperature measured two days ago. The obtained models are relatively stable, and the results show that humidity and precipitation are not significant when considering the high concentrations of *Pm*10.

It is interesting to note that the predictors with the greatest influence in model *M6* after the PM_{10} concentrations measured on the previous day are, in sequence, the minimum temperature from two days ago, followed by the minimum temperature from yesterday, and the minimum temperature from the current day. This undoubtedly shows that the minimum temperature is a major factor in high levels of the air pollutant PM_{10}. In other words, low temperatures require greater consumption of wood and coal for heating households.

The inclusion of the predictor *Pm*10<1> is based on the previous verification using the ARIMA method in this Chapter 4, which found that the high values of PM_{10} concentrations are influenced in terms of autoregression by the values of PM_{10} from a number of previous days (see Figure 4.5).

Precipitation and relative humidity have no influence and can be considered to have a negligible effect on PM_{10} air pollution in Smolyan.

Table 4.6. Relative variable importance of the predictors in selected CART models of pm10 for Smolyan

Predictor	Relative importance scores					
	Model *M1*	Model *M2*	Model *M3*	Model *M4*	Model *M5*	Model *M6*
*Pm*10<1>	100	100	100	100	100	100
minTemp<2>	71.74	74.80	75.00	79.65	75.91	83.74
AP	3.73	-	63.65	-	39.90	-
minTemp<1>	76.68	20.32	56.37	80.65	52.02	55.73
month_day	41.61	35.39	44.84	39.95	44.24	43.82
wthr	18.35	27.93	44.77	11.63	32.48	46.19
WD	3.76	-	23.91	-	13.15	23.20
maxTemp<1>	-	10.50	17.78	-	12.55	26.62
CC	-	-	16.96	-	-	15.87
WS	4.39	-	6.84	-	-	17.53
maxTemp<2>	39.94	33.33	-	13.26	-	-
*month_*	-	30.44	-	-	-	-
minTemp	-	13.73	-	62.00	24.62	52.45
maxTemp	5.50	-	-	12.69	-	-
minTemp<3>	-	-	-	73.03	-	-
prec	-	-	-	-	9.38	-
RH	-	-	-	-	10.10	-

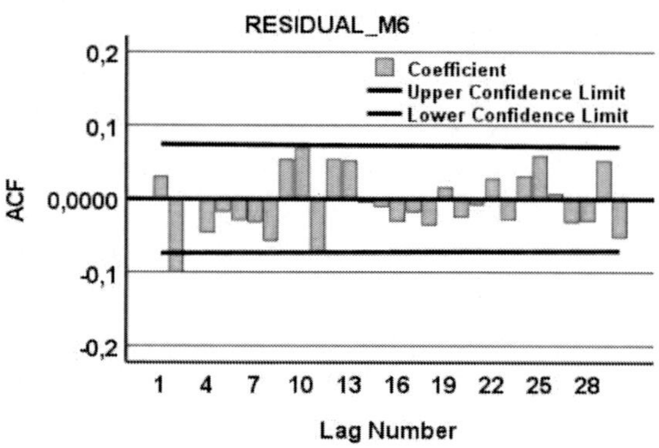

Figure 4.6. ACF of the residuals of the CART model *M3* for Smolyan.

Figure 4.6 shows the autocorrelation function (ACF), which proves the reliability of the selected best model *M6*. It can be noted that the distribution of the residuals falls within the confidence intervals, and this gives reason to consider that the *M6* model is adequate, as there is no autocorrelation in its errors.

Figure 4.7 shows the agreement between the measurements and the predictions from the *M6* model. This is estimated to be around 87% within a 95% confidence interval.

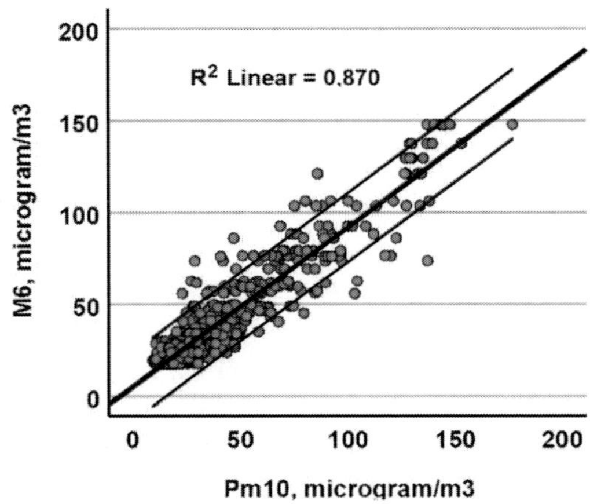

Figure 4.7. Prediction of the CART model *M6* vs. measured PM_{10} data for Smolyan within a 95% confidence interval.

From the obtained statistical results and error diagnosis, it can be concluded that the selected best model *M6* has very good accuracy and is suitable for prediction and forecasting PM_{10} concentrations.

- Application of the CART models for short-term forecasting

CART models have been applied for short-term forecasting of future pollution with *Pm*10 in the town of Smolyan up to 3 days ahead. For this purpose, data from real measurements for the period from 28 April 2018 to 30 April 2018 were used. These data are not included in the analyses, but their levels are compared with the values predicted by the three selected CART models - *M4*, *M5*, and *M6*.

Table 4.7 demonstrates the results of *Pm*10 forecasting with the three selected CART models. Close prediction values are observed for all three models with the actual measured PM_{10} concentrations.

Table 4.7. Comparison between predicted and forecasted PM_{10} values for Smolyan

Date	Measured PM_{10}, μg/m³	Model *M4*, μg/m³	Model *M5*, μg/m³	Model *M6*, μg/m³
25 April 2018	26.21	30.57	28.96	29.84
26 April 2018	29.67	23.86	28.96	29.84
27 April 2018	33.94	30.57	28.96	34.02
28 April 2018	33.95	30.57	28.96	48.87
29 April 2018	26.12	30.57	21.93	18.70
30 April 2018	32.65	23.86	28.96	29.84

Figure 4.8 shows the comparison of the initial data of PM_{10} with the forecasted values from the *M6* model over the last 3 days. The forecasted values of the model are presented as a dotted line, and the continuous line shows the actual measured data of the air pollutant. It can be noted that the predicted values well approximate the original data.

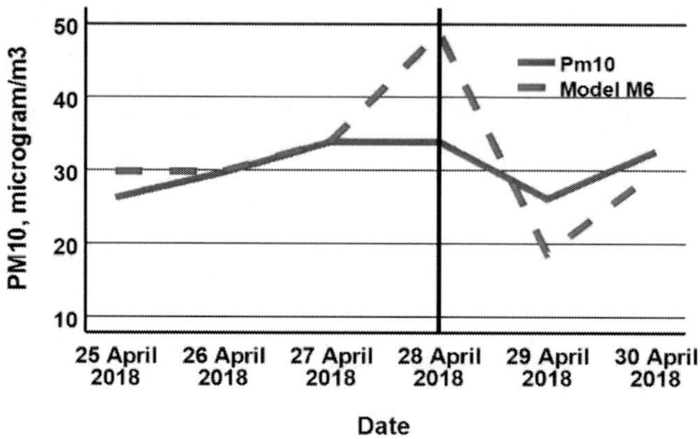

Figure 4.8. Forecasted values from the CART model *M6* compared to the actual measured concentrations of PM_{10} in Smolyan.

Conclusion

The object of study in this chapter is the air pollutant PM_{10} in the town of Smolyan. The selected period for analysis is from 1 January 2010 to 27 April 2018. ARIMA and CART models were applied and compared. From the results presented, we can conclude that the performance of each method is affected to a different degree, depending on the sample size.

For ARIMA models, the obtained statistics are unsatisfactory. The best ARIMA model *A*3=ARIMA/TR(1,1,1) with a sample size of 1520 records fits the actual data with R^2=66.7% and has a RMSE=16.781$\mu g/m^3$. The main influence in this model for each current day is the previous day's values (since the ARIMA parameter p=1). The predictors *minTemp, maxTemp, AP, WS*, and *RH* also influence the model. There is no significant difference in the results of the other three ARIMA models. It should be noted that in ARIMA models, only numerical predictors are used, and string variables are not considered.

Based on the results of the conducted research, it has been demonstrated that with the reduction of the sample size, the quality of the obtained regression CART models improves significantly. The first CART model, *M*4, was built using the entire sample of data for *Pm*10. When building the *M*5 model, the sample was reduced to half of that of *M*4, and the third last CART model, *M*6, was built based on half of the data of *M*5. Very good results were achieved with the CART model *M*6, which reached the highest coefficient of determination R^2=87.02% and had the lowest RMSE=10.181 $\mu g/m^3$. Models *A*2, *A*3 and all CART models showed that fine particulate matter pollution during the current day is most strongly influenced by the measured levels of PM_{10} from the previous day, followed by the minimum temperature measured during the other two previous days. This is explained by slightly stagnant characteristics of meteorological and atmospheric variables in the Smolyan region, located in an area with a hollow relief, the weak wind along the length of the town of 25 km, and low temperatures in the winter period.

The general conclusion is that when modelling time series with ML methods, the sample size should be reduced by including more recent data, as the performance of the model improves and the forecasts are more reliable. We recommend this effective approach for any type of model.

In this study, we empirically show that the sample size can significantly affect the performance of ML techniques, especially the statistical goodness of fit of the regression trees methods.

Part of this study, as reference results are published in [1].

References

[1] Stoimenova-Minova, M. P., Gocheva-Ilieva, S. G. and Ivanov, A. V., 2020, June. PM10 prediction using CART method depending on the number of observations. In *Proceedings of the 2020 3rd International Conference on Mathematics and*

Statistics (ICoMS), ACM International Conference Proceedings Series (ICPS), (pp. 65-70).

[2] Shahraiyni, T. H. and Sodouli, S., 2016. Statistical modeling approaches for PM10 prediction in urban areas: a review of 21st-century studies. *Atmosphere*, 7(2), art. 15.

[3] Stadlober, E., Hörmann, S. and Pfeiler, B., 2008. Quality and performance of a PM10 daily forecasting model. *Atmospheric Environment*, 42, pp. 1098-1109.

[4] Slini, T., Kaprara, A., Karatzas, K. and Moussiopoulos, N., 2006. PM10 forecasting for Thessaloniki, Greece. *Environmental Modelling & Software*, 21(4), pp. 559-565.

[5] Kukkonen, J., Partanen, L., Karppinen, A., Walden, J., Kartastenpää, R., Aarnio, P., Koskentalo, T. and Berkowicz, R., 2003. Evaluation of the OSPM model combined with an urban background model against the data measured in 1997 in Runeberg Street, Helsinki. *Atmospheric Environment*, 37, pp. 1101-1112.

[6] Cohen, J. C., 1988. *Statistical Power Analysis for the Behavioral Sciences.* Routledge, New York.

[7] Ganchev, I., Ji, Z. and O'Droma, M., 2019. Designing a cloud tier for the iot platform EMULSION. *WSEAS Transactions on Systems and Control*, 14, art. 46, pp. 375-383.

[8] IBM SPSS Statistics, https://www.ibm.com/products/spss-statistics

[9] Salford Predictive Modeler (SPM). https://www.minitab.com/en-us/products/spm/

[10] EU air quality standards, 2024. https://environment.ec.europa.eu/topics/air/air-quality/eu-air-quality-standards_en.

[11] Box, G. E. P., Jenkins, G. M., Reinsel, G. S., Ljung, G. M., 2016. *Time Series Analysis, Forecasting and Control*, 5th edn., John Wiley & Sons. Inc, New Jersey.

[12] Mills, T. C., 2019. Applied Time Series Analysis: A Practical Guide to Modeling and Forecasting. Academic Press.

[13] Breiman, L., Friedman, J. H., Stone, C. J. and Olshen, R. A., 1984. Classification and Regression Trees. Chapman & Hall Wadsworth, Inc., New York.

[14] Steinberg, D., 2009. CART: Classification and Regression Trees. In *The top ten algorithms in data mining* (pp. 179-202). Chapman and Hall/CRC.

[15] Yeo, I. K. and Johnson, R. A., 2000. A new family of power transformations to improve normality or symmetry. *Biometrika* 87(4), pp. 954-959.

[16] Dickey, D. A. and Fuller, W. A., 1979. Distribution of the estimators for autoregressive time series with a unit root. *Journal of the American Statistical Association*, 74(366a), pp. 427-431.

[17] Wolfram Mathematica, https://www.wolfram.com/mathematica/.

[18] Steinberg, D. and Golovnya, M., 2007. CART 6.0 User's Guide. *Salford Systems*, San Diego, CA.

[19] Izenman, J., 2008. Modern Multivariate Statistical Techniques. *Regression, Classification, and Manifold Learning.* Springer, New York.

Chapter 5

Forecasting PM_{10} Concentrations Using Random Forests and Arcing Stacked by MARS

Abstract

This study examines the average daily PM_{10} concentrations in Burgas, a region of Bulgaria, near the Black Sea coast, two lakes, and a large refinery for oil and petroleum products. Data on PM_{10} and meteorological variables such as air temperature, humidity, wind speed, and others for a period of 2 years and 4 months are studied. Regression analysis with the Random Forests (RF) and Arcing machine learning (ML) methods is used for statistical modeling of the time series. The built models fit the original pollutant data by more than 95%. The comparison of the models' performance and accuracy shows almost identical indicators for the selected best models, with an advantage for the Arcing models. To improve the forecasting, the selected best models are fitted with the MARS algorithm. This allowed for an increase in the performance of the final model to over 96% match with current data and reduced prediction error. The models are applied for short-term forecasts of PM_{10} concentrations 5 days ahead.

Keywords: arcing, boosting, ensemble trees, forecast, Multivariate adaptive regression splines (MARS), particulate matter, random forest, stacking

5.1. Introduction

Environmental pollution caused by human activity is becoming a serious problem for the health of the population. This situation affects many Bulgarian cities, including those along the Black Sea coast and along the Danube River.

The concentrations of PM_{10}, a primary pollutant, depend on specific meteorological, topographic, industrial, and other conditions for each urban area. The collected measurements allow conducting statistical studies to establish dependencies, trends, and causes of pollution with individual problematic pollutants. This allows for analysis, classifications, and more accurate forecasting of future pollution in both the short and long term. Recent statistical studies have been conducted and published in [1-5], where results have been obtained for the spread of PM_{10} in northern Bulgaria - Ruse and the Danube region. In [6-9], PM_{10} models for other Bulgarian cities located near the Danube River and the Black Sea (Ruse, Nessebar, Burgas) were built and studied, emphasizing ML methods and ARIMA. Some of the algorithms for modeling air pollutants are included in the IoT platform EMULSION for monitoring and improving air quality in Bulgarian cities [10].

In this chapter, we empirically analyze, model, and predict PM_{10} pollution in the town of Burgas. Measured data for PM_{10}, weather, and atmospheric variables are considered stochastic. The results are obtained using the RF, Arcing, and MARS methods by implementing the ML and predictive analytics software of Salford Predictive Modeler (SPM) [11].

5.2. Study Area: The City of Burgas

Burgas is one of the largest cities in Bulgaria. It is the fourth-largest city in Bulgaria with a population of about 200 thousand inhabitants. Burgas is situated on the Black Sea shore, in the region of Northern Thrace. The city is surrounded by the Burgas Lakes and is located at the westernmost point of the Black Sea, at the large Burgas Bay. The city is at a distance of 390 km from the capital Sofia and 130 km from Varna. Burgas is the administrative center of the area with the same name. Near the city is the Southern industrial zone with LUKOIL Neftochim Burgas, the largest oil refinery in the Balkans and the largest industrial enterprise in Bulgaria, and the Northern industrial zone. Pan-European Corridor 8 passes through the city. Burgas is the center of the Bulgarian fishing and fish processing industry (see municipality of Burgas at https://www.burgas.bg/#).

Burgas has a humid subtropical climate (Köppen climate classification Cfa) with continental influences. The climate is strongly influenced by the sea and the flat landscape of the region. The average daily mean temperatures range from 3°C in January to 24°C in August. Summer time sea temperatures vary from 23–30°C, averaging 26°C.

The automatic measuring station is situated in Dolno Ezerovo, Burgas district, with coordinates (42.518892, 27.375144).

5.3. Dataset and Preliminary Data Processing

To perform statistical analyses, official data provided by the Burgas authorities of the Executive Environment Agency (ExEA) [12] are used. The data are on a daily scale, in the period from January 1, 2019, to April 28, 2021, or a total of N=849 days.

The used meteorological variables are as follows: *MaxT*, °C (maximum daily air temperature), *MinT*, °C (minimum daily air temperature), *WindSpeed*, m/s (wind speed), *WindDir$*, categorical (wind direction), *Humidity*, % (relative air humidity), *Pressure*, mbar (atmospheric pressure), *Cloud*, % (cloud conditions), *Rain*, cm.

In addition to these data, we look at additional variables that affect PM_{10}. To describe the data as dynamic and time-dependent, a variable *DAY* with values 1,2, ..., N is used. Along with this, two other independent variables are involved, namely *Season*$ and *PM*10<1>. *Season*$ is of categorical type, with four values (Winter, Spring, Summer, and Autumn). The *PM*10<1> will serve to express the stochastic processes from the previous day, obtained from *PM*10 with one lag back in time. In preliminary studies, it was found that the correlation coefficient Spearman's Rho (*PM*10, *PM*10 <1>) is equal to 0.725, with a significance of p = 0.000. As the correlation is not too strong, the variable *PM*10<1> is suitable as a predictor in regression-type models, such as RF.

The permissible official European and national upper limits for PM_{10} are as follows: daily average up to 50 micrograms per cubic meter, which must not be exceeded more than 35 times within one calendar year, and 40 $\mu g/m^3$ on average per year (see also Table 1.1). The prescribed upper limits by the World Health Organization (WHO) for PM_{10} are: up to 20 $\mu g/m^3$ annually and up to 50 $\mu g/m^3$ daily [13].

Descriptive statistics of the measured numerical type data for Burgas in this chapter are presented in Table 5.1. The categorical variable *WinDir*$, which assumes 16 values corresponding to the geographical direction of the wind, is not included here. The missing values for PM_{10} are 35, which is about 4.1%. The missing values were replaced using the method of linear interpolation, so that the mean value of the variable was not changed. Additionally, there is a single outlier value of 248 $\mu g/m^3$ in the data. It has been replaced by the second largest value, 123 $\mu g/m^3$. The resulting variable is denoted by the same variable *PM*10. From Table 5.1, it is observed that the average value of PM_{10} concentrations for the studied period is 35.69 $\mu g/m^3$. This is close to the upper limits of the prescribed EU and national norms [14].

For observed concentrations of PM_{10}, Table 5.1 shows large values of the coefficients of Skewness (3.615) and Kurtosis (33.760), with correspondingly low coefficients for their standard errors. We can conclude that the distribution of the initial target variable $PM10$ is not normal.

Table 5.1. Descriptive statistics of the measured data for Burgas

Statistic	*PM*10 $\mu g/m^3$	*MaxT*, °C	*MinT*, °C	*WindSpeed*, m/s	*Humidity*, %	*Pressure*, mbar	*Cloud*, %	*Rain*, cm
N valid	814	849	849	849	849	846	849	849
N missing	35	0	0	0	0	3	0	0
Mean	35.69	16.75	10.25	12.66	71.78	1017	36.8	1.855
Median	32.12	15.00	10.00	11.00	72.00	1016	30.00	8.00
Std. Deviation	16.779	8.116	6.707	5.586	9.265	6.958	28.917	5.248
Variance	281.55	65.88	44.98	31.20	85.85	48.416	836.2	27.54
Skewness	3.615	0.076	-0.036	1.344	-0.156	0.156	0.629	4.978
Std. Error of Skewness	0.086	0.084	0.084	0.084	0.084	0.084	0.084	0.084
Kurtosis	33.760	-1.079	-1.020	2.847	-0.305	0.134	-0.759	29.24
Std. Error of Kurtosis	0.171	0.168	0.168	0.168	0.168	0.168	0.168	0.168
Minimum	5	-1	-7	3	42	990	0	0
Maximum	248	33	24	41	96	1040	100	49.7

Figure 5.1 illustrates the sequence plot of the variable $PM10$, where the horizontal dashed line with values 50 $\mu g/m^3$ indicates the daily permissible upper limit according to European and national standards for this pollutant. It can be concluded that the state of clean air in Burgas is not good and remains problematic for PM_{10}, especially during the winter months. Figure 5.1 also shows a continuously high background pollution up to and below the average daily allowable limit of 50 $\mu g/m^3$ and values many times exceeding the lower WHO prescriptions.

Figures 5.2(a) and (b) illustrate the time series of the minimum and maximum daily temperatures for the studied time period, and Figure 5.3(c) represents the wind speed values. A clear inverse relationship between temperatures and PM_{10} concentrations is observed. The relationship between wind speed and PM_{10} is direct. We can expect that meteorological variables have a significant impact on PM_{10} levels.

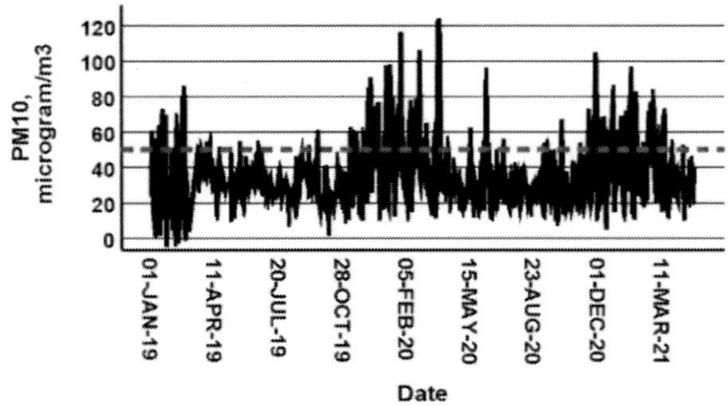

Figure 5.1. Sequence plot of the measured daily concentrations of PM_{10} in Burgas, Bulgaria. The horizontal dashed line points out the permissible daily limit value of $50\ \mu g/m^3$ for PM_{10} according to European and national standards.

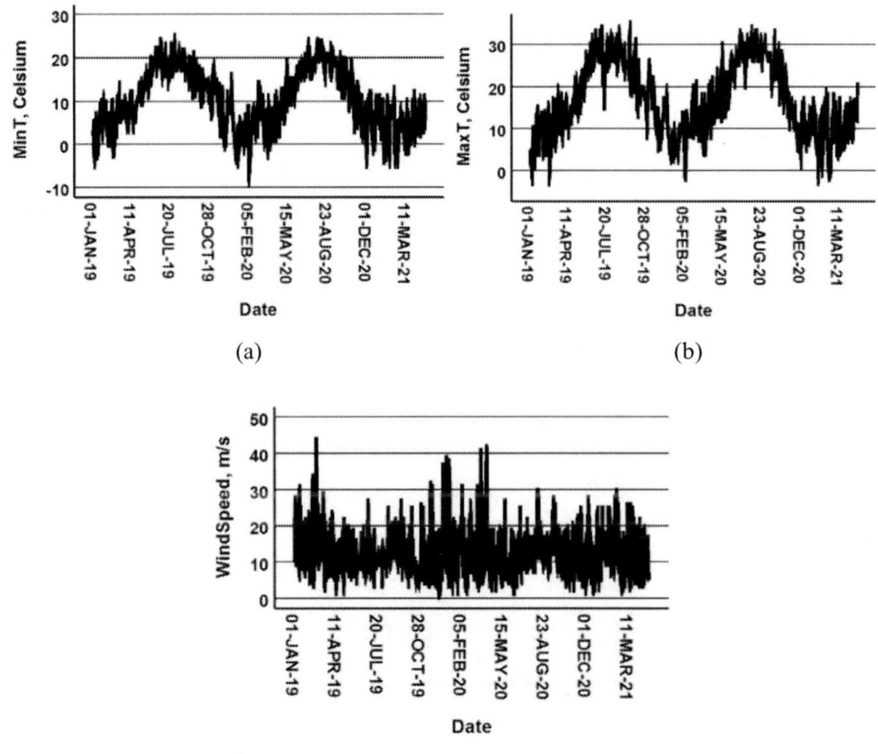

Figure 5.2. Sequence plots of the initial data for Burgas: (a) minimum average daily air temperature *MinT*, °C; (b) maximum average daily air temperature *MaxT*, °C; (c) average daily wind speed, m/s.

In fact, the *PM*10 variable contain both a deterministic and a stochastic component. In the latter, additional influences are implicitly included, which may not be measured. For this reason, the use of several lagged variables is essential.

To improve the *PM*10 distribution towards normal, we perform the inverse hyperbolic sine transformation as follows:

$$t_{PM10} = sinh^{-1}(x) = \ln\left(x + \sqrt{x^2 + 1}\right), \quad x = PM10. \tag{5.1}$$

The transformed variable *t_PM*10 has the following improved coefficients: Skewness = -0.321 with Std. Err. of Skewness = 0.084 and Kurtosis = 2.348 with Std. Err. of Kurtosis = 0.168. The corresponding statistics of the Kolmogorov-Smirnov test with the Lilliefors significance correction are equal to 0.113 and 0.044 for *PM*10 and *t_PM*10, respectively.

The result before and after the transformation is shown in Figure 5.3.

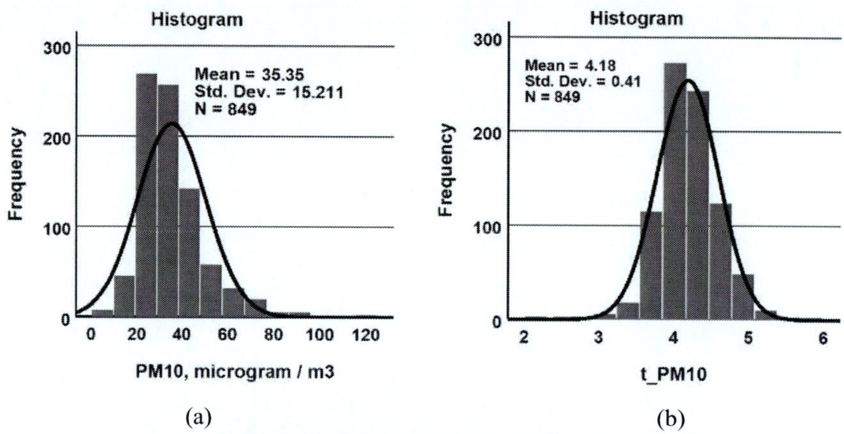

Figure 5.3. Histograms: (a) of the initial variable *PM*10; (b) of the transformed variable *t_PM*10.

In further analyses of this chapter, the transformed variable *t_PM*10 is modeled. After receiving the models, the results are retransformed back to the original data with the expression

$$x = sinh(y). \tag{5.2}$$

We use the Random Forests and Arcing algorithms of Salford Predictive Modeler analysis engines to construct models and predict PM_{10} values [11]. RF and Arcing methods are presented in Chapter 3.

5.4. Building RF Models of PM_{10}

The first goal is to build regression RF models - to determine the relationship between the *t_PM*10 as dependent variable and the 13 independent variables: 7 variables described in Table 5.1 (*MinT, MaxT, WindSpeed, Humidity, Pressure*, *Cloud, Rain*), *DAY* (ordinal), two categorical *WinDir*$ and *Season*$, and the three lagged variables *t_PM*10<1>, *t_PM*10<2>, and *t_PM*10<3>.

The hyperparameter T for the number of regression trees in the RF ensembles is set to 200. The minimum number in the terminal node's values is 2 and 5, denoted in the models as *a*2 and *a*5, respectively. The maximum number of samples redraws is *mtry*=3. The training of the models is carried out with the standard well-proven procedure called out-of-bag (OOB) - random test sample, which is about *N*/3 in size [15].

Figure 5.4 shows an example of mean squared error (MSE) against the number of trees T. In fact, the minimum value of the error at T=200 has not been reached, but the MSE decreases very slowly. For this reason, we built models with a fixed T=200 trees.

Two RF models have been selected to predict the target variable *t_PM*10, from which the last 5 values have been removed and will serve to assess the predictive properties of the models. This variable is denoted by *t_PM*10_5.

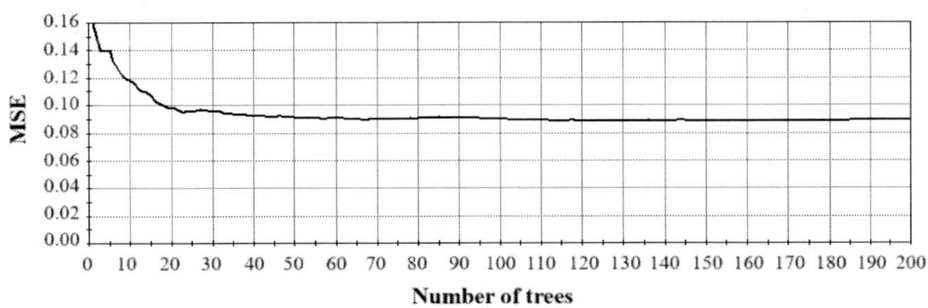

Figure 5.4. MSE error curve as a function of the number of ensemble trees for the case T = 200 in RF models.

Table 5.2. Summary statistics of the selected RF models of PM_{10}

Model	Sample	R^2	IA	RMSE	MAE	MAPE	MBE	DW
*reM*1, *reRF*200*a*5	Whole	0.9041	0.9460	6.0347	3.8206	10.99%	1.5069	1.483
	Learn	0.9046	0.9462	6.0401	3.8260	10.97%	1.5121	1.482
	Test	-	0.7194	5.0293	4.4814	14.13%	0.6153	-
*reM*2, *reRF*200*a*2	Whole	0.9450	0.9534	5.5830	3.3722	9.49%	1.5291	1.404
	Learn	0.9457	0.9536	5.5837	3.3751	9.46%	1.5357	1.397
	Test	-	0.6452	5.4519	4.5631	14.59%	0.4165	-

Table 5.2 presents summary statistics for two selected RF models for retransformed predicted values. Model *M*1 was grown with T = 200 trees, a2 = 5. Model *M*2 was built with T = 200 trees, a5 = 5. The statistics of the two models, calculated after retransformation, are very close, with the second *reM*2 slightly superior to the first, mainly due to a higher coefficient of determination (R^2).

The relative importance of all predictors in these models is given in Table 5.3. A stable distribution is observed. The highest score (100) is that of the lagged variable *t_PM*10<1>, which takes into account the impact of PM_{10} concentrations from the previous day. The variable importance of *DAY, WindSpeed, MinT, Seasons*\$, *MaxT,* and *WinDir*\$ follows in descending order. Other predictors have less influence. In model *M*2, Seasons\$ takes the third position.

Table 5.3. Relative variable importance in the selected RF models

Variable	Model *M*1	Model *M*2
*t_PM*10<1>	100.00	100.00
DAY	16.97	18.56
WinDir\$	10.17	8.14
MinT	9.57	14.57
MaxT	8.80	10.40
Rain	7.90	8.00
*t_PM*10<2>	7.68	8.61
WindSpeed	4.46	7.87
Cloud	4.43	5.05
Season\$	3.50	10.64
Weather\$	2.30	4.00
Humidity	1.35	1.67
Pressure	0.41	1.19
*t_PM*10<3>	0	0

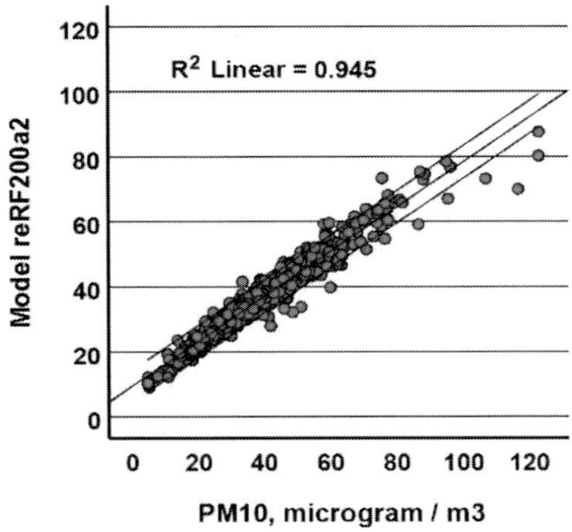

Figure 5.5. Predictions of *reM2* (*reRF200a2*) model against measured PM_{10} concentrations in Burgas with 95% confidence interval.

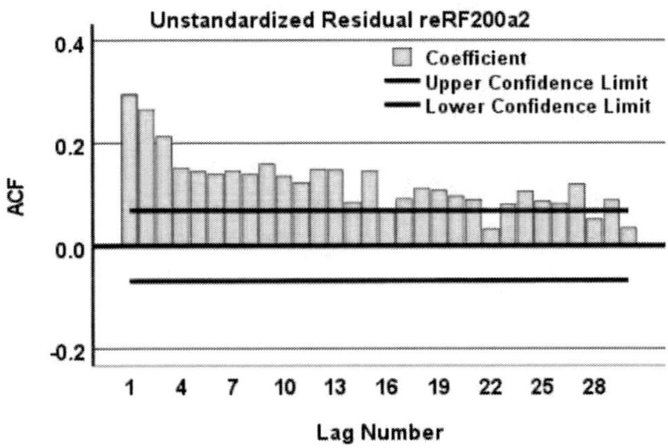

Figure 5.6. ACF plot of the residuals of the *reM2* (*reRF200a2*) model with 95% confidence interval.

Figure 5.5 shows the predicted values from model *reM2*, *reRF200a2*, after retransformation against measured PM_{10} values. This figure shows that despite the large value of the coefficient of determination R^2=0.945, the model *reM2* does not predict the maximum values of PM_{10} well. The latter is a common disadvantage of ensemble techniques due to the averaged values in the tree nodes.

- Analysis of the residuals of RF models

The next Figure 5.6 illustrates the sequence plot of the autocorrelation function (ACF) of the residuals of the *reM2* model. Multiple coefficient values outside the confidence interval are observed. This indicates the presence of autocorrelation in the model. The use of the model for forecasting may only be conditional. This disagreement could be resolved using an ARIMA error correction model.

5.5. Arcing Models

The other approach to modeling the data for Burgas uses the Arcing method. We use the same 11 predictors and two lagged variables of the target variable *t_PM*10_5. Following the procedure for the RF models, we get the corresponding results with Arcing.

After varying the values of the hyperparameters, the Arcing models were selected as follows: number of trees in the ensemble 30 and 40; minimum number of observations in the parent node of a tree m1=5; minimum number of observations in the child node m2=5. The maximum number of sample redraws is 3. Model training is performed using the standard 10-fold cross-validation procedure (see Chapter 3). Table 5.4 presents the summary statistics of the two selected Arcing models after retransformation of the predicted values.

Table 5.4. Summary statistics of the selected Arcing models of *PM*10

Model	Sample	R^2	IA	RMSE	MAE	MAPE	MBE	DW
reM3 (*reARC*30)	Whole	0.9491	0.9772	4.1948	3.1688	8.82%	1.1917	1.940
	Learn	0.9500	0.9774	4.1849	3.1607	8.77%	1.1986	1.931
	Test	-	0.6127	5.6172	5.1196	16.89%	0.0338	-
*reM*4 (*reARC*40)	Whole	0.9551	0.9791	4.0203	3.0221	8.37%	1.1604	1.948
	Learn	0.9559	0.9794	4.0100	3.0134	8.32%	1.1689	1.939
	Test	-	0.6126	5.4868	5.0501	16.76%	-0.2734	-

From Table 5.4, the best statistics come out for the re*M*4 model. This model also shows slightly better performance compared to the RF models in Table 5.2.

The relative influence of all predictors in the constructed models is presented in Table 5.5. In the *M*4 Arcing model, the highest score of 100 is assigned to the lagged variable *t_PM*10<1>. Then, in descending order, the scores of *Weather*$ (54), *WinDir*$ (51), *Day* (47), *t_PM10*<2> (45), etc., are evaluated. This is mainly explained by the mutual correlation of the predictors, as well as the difference in the algorithms of the two methods. In essence, a good degree of diversity is obtained indirectly, which is considered an essential requirement for stacking [16 - 18].

Table 5.5. Relative weight of predictors in the two best Arcing models

Variable	Model *M*3	Model *M*4
*t_PM*10_5<1>	100.00	100.00
DAY	46.6	47.2
WinDir$	51.3	51.1
MinT	27.4	29.2
MaxT	30.2	32.4
Rain	19.2	23.1
*t_PM*10_5<2>	45.0	46.0
WindSpeed	28.2	28.0
Cloud	24.3	27.5
Season$	13.0	12.6
Weather$	54.1	54.1
Humidity	20.0	23.0
Pressure	25.1	23.1
*t_PM*10_5<3>	31.7	32.3

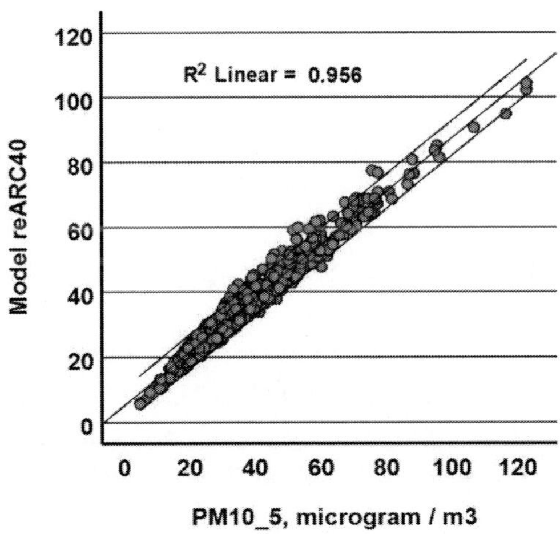

Figure 5.7. Predictions of the *reM*4 (*reARC*40) model versus actual PM_{10} data with 95% confidence interval.

Figure 5.7 shows the predicted values from model *reM*4 (*reARC*40) after retransformation against measured PM_{10} values. More accurate predictions of high PM_{10} values are observed compared to the predictions of the RF model *reM*2.

- Analysis of the residuals of Arcing models

The following Figure 5.8 shows the autocorrelation function (ACF) plot of the residuals of the *reM*4 model, *reARC*40. In this case, no ACF coefficients are observed outside the confidence interval. We can assume that the model does not contain a serial correlation and is adequate. It can be used to predict the PM_{10} time series.

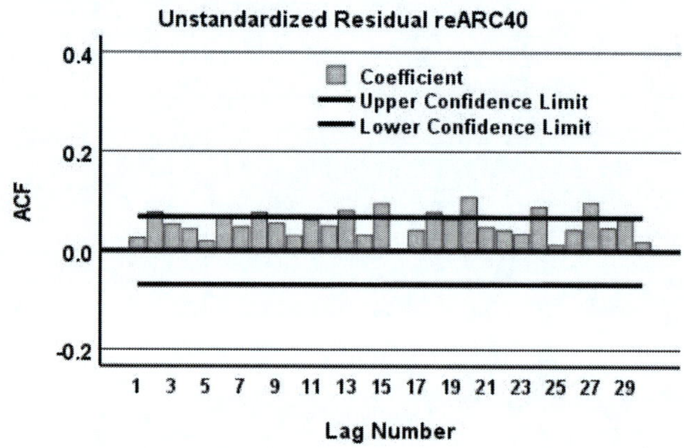

Figure 5.8. ACF plot of the residuals of the model *reM*4 (*reARC*40).

5.6. Stacking Random Forests and Arcing Models by MARS

The obtained N = 849 predicted values of *t_PM*10 with models *M*2 and *M*4 will be stacked using the Multivariate Adaptive Regression Splines (MARS) method [19] (see also Ch. 3). In this case, *M*2 and *M*4 are in the role of base models (or predictors), which are stacked at the meta-level with the MARS model.

The following hyperparameters were used to construct MARS models: M_0- maximum number of basis functions (BFs), *r*- degree of interactions between predictors, and a 10-fold cross-validation procedure. After varying the values of M_0 between 10, 15, 20, and *r* - 0 and 1, two MARS models were selected. At r=0, the model is linear and contains BFs only of the first degree. We denote it with *S*1 (*sMARS*1). For r=1, the model contains members up to the second degree. In this case, its notation is *S*2 (*sMARS*2). BFs and MARS equations are presented in (5.3) - (5.4) for the linear model *S*1 and (5.5) - (5.6) for *S*2, respectively.

The stacked linear *S*1 model *sMARS*1 is written as

$$\begin{aligned} &BF1 = max(0, ARC40 - 3.84367);\\ &BF2 = \max(0, 3.84367 - ARC40);\\ &BF4 = \max(0, 4.63823 - RF200a2); \end{aligned} \tag{5.3}$$

$$\begin{aligned} sMARS1 = 3.67395 + 1.26492 * BF1\\ -1.15649 * BF2 + 0.198889 * BF4 \end{aligned} \tag{5.4}$$

The second-order model *sMARS*2 has the form

$$\begin{aligned} &BF1 = \max(0, ARC40 - 3.84367);\\ &BF2 = \max(0, 3.84367 - ARC40);\\ &BF4 = \max(0, 4.63823 - RF200a2);\\ &BF6 = \max(0, RF200a2 - 3.99262);\\ &BF7 = \max(0, 3.99262 - RF200a2);\\ &BF8 = \max(0, ARC40 - 3.05935) * BF7;\\ &BF10 = \max(0, ARC40 - 2.46331) * BF4;\\ &BF11 = \max(0, RF200a2 - 3.27725); \end{aligned} \tag{5.5}$$

$$\begin{aligned} &sMARS2 = 3.78548 + 1.21122 * BF1\\ &-1.06264 * BF2 + 0.339138 * BF6\\ &- 0.260524 * BF8 + 0.179223 * BF10\\ &-0.224855 * BF11 \end{aligned} \tag{5.6}$$

In (5.5) - (5.6), eight BFs are involved, of which 6 remain in the final formula of *sMARS*2. From the second degree are the two functions *BF*8 and *BF*10.

The statistical indicators of the two stacked models are given in Table 5.6. After retransforming the values, the models are denoted by *reS*1 and *reS*2, respectively. The achieved goodness-of-fit measures are superior to the corresponding values of the *reM*2 and *reM*4 models. From Table 5.6, you can see that the two stacked models, *reS*1 and *reS*2, have very close indicators. A coefficient of determination R^2 of over 96%, and an MAPE of 0.02% was obtained. To check the lack of autocorrelation of errors on these models, the Durbin-Watson (DW) test was used. The DW values for the four models are close to 2. It follows that the models do not contain a significant autocorrelation. In addition, to check for autocorrelation, Figure 5.9 shows the autocorrelation functions (ACF) of the residuals of the two models *reS*1 and *reS*2. It is observed that all coefficients are within the limits of confidence intervals. We can conclude that there is no autocorrelation in the residuals, and the models follow the white noise requirements.

Almost identical statistical indicators of *reS*1 and *reS*2 were obtained. Following the parsimony principle [20], we will choose *reS*1 as a better model.

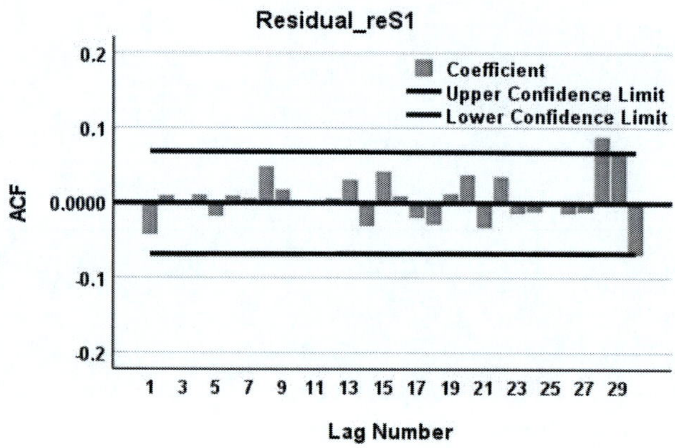

(a)

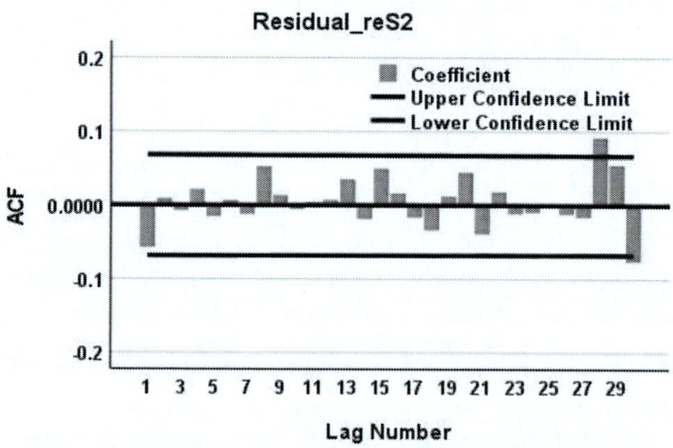

(b)

Figure 5.9. ACF plots of the residuals for the two stacked MARS models (a) *reS*1 and (b) *reS*2.

Table 5.6. Summary statistics of the selected stacked MARS models of PM_{10}

Model	R^2	IA	RMSE	MAE	MAPE	MBE	DW
*reS*1 (*sMARS*1)	0.9613	0.9901	3.0004	2.3769	6.99%	0.0932	2.036
*reS*2 (*sMARS*2)	0.9614	0.9901	2.9908	2.3646	6.89%	0.1020	2.064

The variable importance of the two predictor models *M*2 (*RF200a*2) and *M*4 (*ARC*40) in the stacked models is given in Table 5.7. The influence of Arcing is dominant in both models.

Table 5.7. Relative variable importance in the stacked MARS models

Variable (model predictor)	Model *S*1, *sMARS*1	Model *S*2, *sMARS*2
*M*4, *ARC*40	100.00	100.00
*M*2, *RF*200*a*2	12.30	12.47

5.7. Short-Time Forecasts

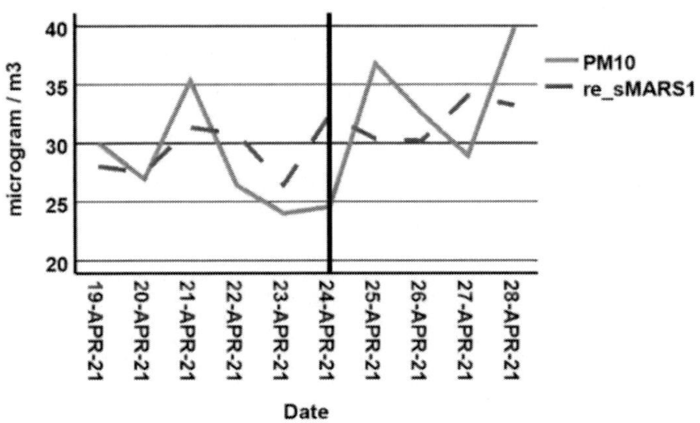

Figure 5.10. Measured PM_{10} for the last 10 days against the modeled *PM*10 concentrations in Burgas using the best stacked MARS model *reS*1 (*re_sMARS*1). To the left of the vertical line are the values predicted by the model, and to the right are the forecasts of the values that were not used in the modeling procedures.

We will demonstrate and compare the forecasts from the built models with the original data from the holdout test sample. We chose the stacked model *reS*1 (*re_sMARS*1). Figure 5.10 presents the measured PM_{10} data against the predictions of this model for the last 10 days of the study period. Of these, to the right of the middle vertical line are the forecasts for five days, the values of which were not used in the modeling process.

Figure 5.10 shows the same type of behavior of the *reS*1 model for both the 'known' values for the period 19 to 23 August 2021 and for the 'unknown' test values from 24 to 28 August 2021. No significant deviations are observed. We can consider the models to be adequate, and the approach used to be promising for the analysis and forecasting of time series.

Conclusion

The data from measurements of average daily PM_{10} concentrations in Burgas, located on the Black Sea coast of Bulgaria, are processed and analyzed. The investigated data cover a period of 2 years and 4 months, from 1st January 2019 to 28th April 2021.

Modeling is performed using three ML methods – Random Forests, Arcing, and MARS. Four best models were selected, built by RF and Arcing algorithms. The resulting predicted values are then stacked at the meta-level with MARS. The relative importance of all predictors in the RF and Arcing models was determined. The models show that the stochastic type lagged variable *PM*10<1> (from the previous day) has the strongest influence, followed by the day, wind speed, minimum daily temperature, weather conditions, etc.

The models were applied for short-term forecasting of PM_{10} for 5 days ahead. The comparison between the best RF model and the best Arcing model showed that the statistical indicators – a coefficient of determination of 95.5% and the RMSE of the Arcing model are superior to those of the RF model. After the meta-analyses with MARS, all statistical indicators were further improved. Better performance of stacked models was achieved with up to $R^2 = 96\%$, MAPE 0.02%. Excellent results were also achieved in predicting the test sample.

References

[1] Zheleva, I., Veleva, E. and Filipova, M., 2017, October. Analysis and modeling of daily air pollutants in the city of Ruse, Bulgaria. In *AIP Conference Proceedings* (Vol. 1895, No. 1). AIP Publishing.

[2] Tsvetanova, I., Zheleva, I., Filipova, M. and Stefanova, A., 2018. Statistical analysis of ambient air PM10 contamination during winter periods for Ruse region, Bulgaria. In *MATEC Web of Conferences* (Vol. 145, p. 01007). EDP Sciences.

[3] Veleva, E. and Zheleva, I., 2018. Statistical modeling of particle matter air pollutants in the city of Ruse, Bulgaria. In *MATEC Web of Conferences* (Vol. 145, p. 01010). EDP Sciences.

[4] Filipova, M., Zheleva, I. and Roussev, P., 2013. Characteristics of PM air pollution along Bulgaria - Romania Danube region, *Ecologica*, 71, pp. 215-217.

[5] Filipova M., I. Zheleva, P. Rusev, D. Stefanova and I. Tsvetanova, Analysis of the state of ambient air in the border region Bulgaria -Romania. In *Proceedings of the International Symposium Environment and Industry* (SIMI, Bucharest, 2016), (pp. 440-450).

[6] Gocheva-Ilieva, S., Voynikova, D., Stoimenova, M., Ivanov, A. and Iliev, I., 2019. Regression trees modeling of time series for air pollution analysis and forecasting. *Neural Computing and Applications*, 31(12), pp. 9023-9039.

[7] Gocheva-Ilieva, S., Voynikova, D., Ivanov, A. and Stoimenova, M., 2019, October. Two-step time series analysis for air pollution in relation to weather conditions: Case study of Nessebar, Bulgaria. In *AIP Conference Proceedings* (Vol. 2164, No. 1). AIP Publishing.

[8] Gocheva-Ilieva, S. G., Ivanov, A. V. and Stoimenova-Minova, M. P., 2022. Prediction of daily mean PM10 concentrations using random forest and CART ensemble and bagging stacked by MARS. *Sustainability*, 14(2), art. 798.

[9] Koleva, S. K., Gocheva-Ilieva, S. G. and Kulina, H. N., 2023, December. Stochastic modelling of daily air pollution in Burgas, Bulgaria. In *Journal of Physics: Conference Series* (Vol. 2675, No. 1, p. 012003). IOP Publishing.

[10] Ganchev, I., Ji, Z. and O'Droma, M., 2019. Designing a cloud tier for the iot platform EMULSION. *WSEAS Transactions on Systems and Control,* 14, art. 46, pp. 375-383.

[11] Salford Predictive Modeler (SPM). https://www.minitab.com/en-us/products/spm/.

[12] Executive Environment Agency (ExEA), Bulgaria. http://eea.government.bg/en

[13] WHO global air quality guidelines: Particulate matter (PM2.5 and PM10), ozone, nitrogen dioxide, sulfur dioxide and carbon monoxide, 2021. https://iris.who.int/bitstream/handle/10665/345329/9789240034228-eng.pdf.

[14] EU air quality standards, 2024. https://environment.ec.europa.eu/topics/air/air-quality/eu-air-quality-standards_en.

[15] Breiman, L., 2001. Random forests. *Machine Learning*, 45(1), pp. 5-32.

[16] Kuncheva, L. I. and Whitaker, C. J., 2003. Measures of diversity in classifier ensembles and their relationship with the ensemble accuracy. *Machine learning*, 51, pp. 181-207.

[17] Kuncheva, L. I., 2004. *Combining Pattern Classifiers: Methods and Algorithms*. John Wiley and Sons, Inc., Hoboken.

[18] Zhou, Z. H., 2012. *Ensemble Methods: Foundations and Algorithms*. CRC Press, Boca Raton.

[19] Friedman, J. H., 1991. Multivariate adaptive regression splines (with discussion). *Annals of Statistics*, 19(1), pp. 1-141.

[20] Sober, E., 1981. The principle of parsimony. *The British Journal for the Philosophy of Science*, 32(2), pp. 145-156.

Chapter 6

Hybrid Random Forests-ARIMA Modeling of PM_{10} Concentrations

Abstract

A hybrid method has been proposed for the analysis and prediction of atmospheric air pollution with particulate matter PM_{10}, depending on meteorological conditions. The approach is based on Random Forests (RF) and the correction of errors using the ARIMA transfer function Box-Jenkins methodology. Both methods are applied to model data collected over five years for the town of Haskovo, Bulgaria. The Random Forests model was trained using the out-of-bag procedure. The examination of the autocorrelation function of the residuals from the RF model showed the presence of a serial correlation. To eliminate these unwanted errors, the ARIMA method is used. Thus, a statistically adequate hybrid RF_ARIMA-error model was obtained. A model fit of over 85% is achieved, along with a very good prediction of high PM_{10} values.

Keywords: ARIMA error, hybrid model, Random Forests, machine learning, particulate matter, transfer functions

6.1. Initial Data and Data Processing for the City of Haskovo

This case study presents a hybrid approach to modelling PM_{10} concentrations depending on a large number of predictors, such as the weather, minimum and maximum air temperature. The approach involves the use of the Random Forests (RF) method, developed in [1]. An additional adjustment of its residuals, called error correction, is performed by the Box-Jenkins ARIMA methodology [2]. This way, a hybrid model combines the RF tree ensemble and ARIMA with transfer functions (ARIMA/TF) [3]. The objective is to construct a model with enhanced predictive capabilities. The proposed approach is tested using actual empirical data. The computations have been carried out using the Salford-Systems Predictive Modeler and SPSS statistical software [4].

6.1.1. Study Area: The City of Haskovo

Haskovo is the main city in the province of Haskovo, with a population of 70000. It is situated in Southern Bulgaria, close to the Turkish and Greek borders. The terrain is characterized by low hills. The climate in the region is transitional with continental influence to the north and Mediterranean to the south. Haskovo is a center of construction, the food industry, machine building, the chemical industry, wine, food, beverage, and tobacco production, among others.

6.1.2. Data and Data Pre-Processing

The examined data are in the form of time series with average daily measurements of the PM_{10} pollutant and the meteorological variables over the period between 1 January 2015 and 30 September 2019. The sample size is N= 1733.

The target variable for PM_{10} is denoted by $pm10$ $(\mu g/m^3)$. The ten variables used as predictors are as follows: *Tmax* (°C) – maximum daily air temperature, *Tmin* (°C) – minimum daily air temperature, *WSpeed* (m/s) – wind speed, *X*1 and *X*2 are the two polar coordinates of the wind direction with radius 1, *Weather* – coded from "sunny" (0%) to "heavy snow" (100%), and *Cloud* (%) – cloud condition, *Humidity* (%) – relative humidity, and meteorological variables *Precip* (mm) - precipitation and *Pressure* (mbar). The descriptive statistics of all considered variables are given in Table 6.1.

The dependent variable $pm10$ has 175 missing values, or about 10%. In the conducted analyses, these are replaced with linear interpolation, and the same variable name will be used. All other ten variables have no missing values.

From Table 6.1, it is seen that the PM_{10} concentrations achieve high values with a maximum of 264 $\mu g/m^3$ The average concentration of PM_{10} for the examined period of nearly 5 years is 36.9 $\mu g/m^3$.

Figure 6.1 shows the changes in concentrations with relatively high values of PM_{10} during winter and low ones during summer. Permanent exceedances are seen above the European standards' daily allowance for PM$_{10}$ emissions of 50 $\mu g/m^3$ [5], indicated by a dashed line.

Table 6.1. Descriptive statistics of the observed initial data set for Haskovo

Variables	Mean	Median	Minimum	Maximum	Variance	Std. Deviation
$pm10, \mu g/m^3$	36.9	26.60	3	264	964.01	31.049
TMin, °C	9.1	9.1	-15	25	55.675	7.462
TMax, °C	19.49	20.00	-8	41	98.629	9.931
$WSpeed, m/s$	8.89	8.00	1	37	16.128	4.016
*X*1	0.073	0.000	-1	1	0.479	0.692
*X*2	-0.378	-0.707	-1	1	0.374	0.611
Weather, %	0.093	0.000	0	0.95	0.02	0.141
Cloud, %	0.336	0.250	0	1	0.075	0.273
Humidity, %	0.656	0.660	0.28	0.99	0.024	0.154
Precip, mm	1.039	0.000	0	32.1	9.048	3.008
Pressure, mbar	1016.53	1016.00	992	1039	45.983	6.781

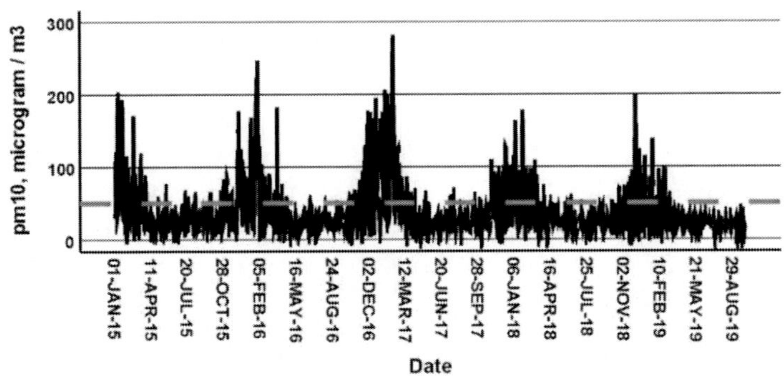

Figure 6.1. Sequence plot of initial PM$_{10}$ data for Haskovo, Bulgaria.

6.2. Applied Hybrid Approach

The modelling is carried out in two main steps.

- Step 1. The first step is to build an RF regression model with the available predictors. Time series of meteorological, atmospheric, their lagged variables, and other time series, as well as a time-varying variable, can be used as predictors. In our case, these are given in Table 6.1. After constructing the RF model, *RES_RF* residuals are calculated. Time series of the residuals are examined to identify outliers and possible autocorrelation. As a result of the regression model, residuals should exhibit white noise behavior with a distribution close to normal. In general, RF models have the aforementioned properties.

- Step 2. In the second step, the residuals *RES_RF* are considered as a dependent variable and are modeled with ARIMA/TF using the initial predictors. We will denote the errors of this model as *RES_HYB*, which gives the error of the final hybrid model.

In this way, the resulting model and its error time series *RES_HYB* take the form:

$$\widehat{H}ybrid = RF + ARIMA(p, d, q),$$
$$RES\_HYB = pm10 - \widehat{H}ybrid. \tag{6.1}$$

The usual goodness-of-fit measures are used in the process of model evaluation and selection of the two types of models mentioned in the two steps above (see (2.12) - (2.16)).

6.3. The Building and Selection of the RF Models

Following step 1, for building RF models, we used the ten predictors, presented in Table 6.1, and a time variable t – the index of the current day, with values from 1 to N. Various models were constructed, and the best one was selected based on statistical performance measures from formulas (2.12)-(2.16). The selected *RF* model was built with the following control parameters: minimum cases in parent node of each tree of the ensemble equal to 10; maximum trees to build the model - 200; out-of-bag (OOB) data are used for testing.

Table 6.2. Summary statistics of the selected RF-ARIMA/TF models of PM_{10} for Haskovo

Model	Dependent variable	R^2	RMSE	Ljung-Box significance statistics
RF model	*pm*10	0.826	14.068	-
ARIMA/TF(3,0,17)	*RES_RF*	0.281	11.995	0.187
$Hybrid\ RF - ARIMA$	*pm*10	0.860	12.019	-

The summary statistics for the best-performing *RF* model are given in the first row of Table 6.2. It was achieved a coefficient of determination $R^2 = 0.826$. This result means that the model explains about 82.6% of the examined data. The Durbin-Watson statistic is close to 2, which indicates there is no high autocorrelation in the error term and the model is consistent.

Figure 6.2 shows the predictions of $pm10$, calculated using the selected *RF model*. It should be noted that despite the relatively high coefficient of determination, the highest values are not well predicted. PM_{10} below $175\ \mu g/m^3$ is reached for a maximum of $264\ \mu g/m^3$.

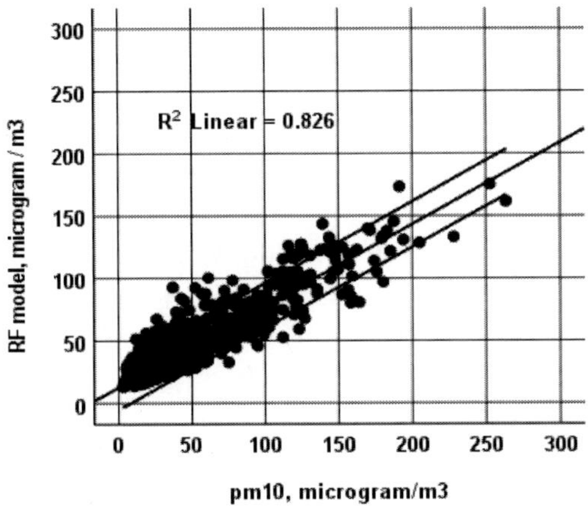

Figure 6.2. *Pm*10 values compared with the predictions obtained using the *RF model*.

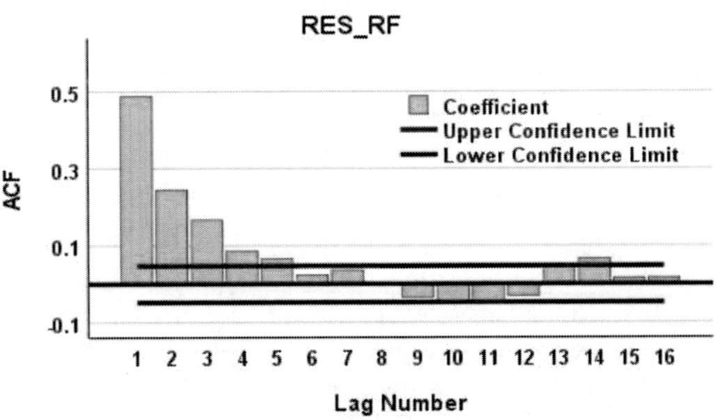

(a)

Figure 6.3. (Continued).

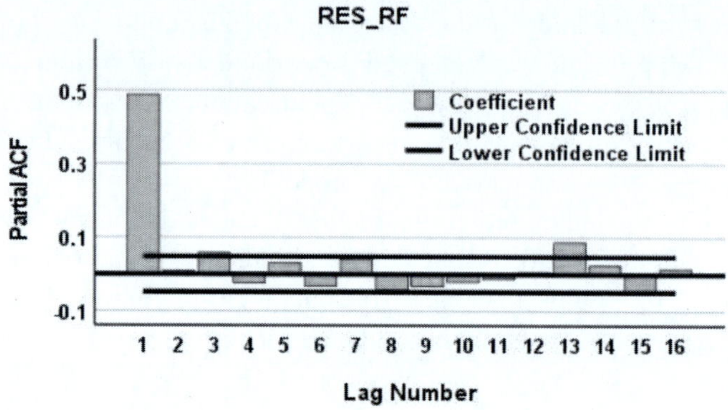

(b)

Figure 6.3. ACF and PACF of residuals of the *RF model* at step 1 with a 95% confidence interval.

The sequence charts of the ACF and PACF of residuals *RES_RF* are shown in Figure 6.3. Several large deviations outside the confidence intervals are observed. From this figure, it can be concluded that the residuals are not satisfactory and they need to be further corrected by performing step 2, as pointed out in subsection 6.2.

6.4. The Building and Analysis of the ARIMA-Error Model

To construct the correction model with ARIMA for the dependent variable *RES_RF*, the ten initial predictors with parameters (p, d, q) and possible delay parameter were used. When we use predictors, the model is of the ARIMA/Transfer function type [2].

The resulting model for our residual data is *ARIMA/TF*(3,0,17). Model statistics are given in the second row of Table 6.2. The Ljung-Box statistics are insignificant with p-value 0.187 > 0.05; therefore, no serial correlation in the residuals of the ARIMA model is detected. Parameters of the *ARIMA/TF*(3,0,17) model for the dependent time series *RES_RF* are presented in Table 6.3. Only estimates for the significant variables and their parameters at a significance level (Sig.) of 0.05 are shown. We will note that the model does not include the variable *Tmin*, which is insignificant. This can be explained by a strong correlation between *Tmax* and *Tmin*.

Table 6.3. Parameters of the *ARIMA model* of *RES_RF* for Haskovo data

Variable	Component	Lag	Estimate	Std. Err.	*t* statistic	Sig.
RE_RF	Constant		-264.594	65.357	-4.048	0.000
	AR	Lag 1	0.465	0.022	21.132	0.000
		Lag 3	0.049	0.022	2.218	0.027
	MA	Lag 1	-0.067	0.024	-2.788	0.005
		Lag 14	-0.096	0.024	-3.940	0.000
		Lag 17	0.067	0.024	2.768	0.006
Tmax	Numerator	Lag 0	0.508	0.088	5.780	0.000
		Lag 2	0.451	0.086	5.261	0.000
Cloud	Numerator	Lag 0	4.389	1.476	2.973	0.003
		Lag 2	5.489	1.437	3.819	0.000
Weather	Delay		1			
	Numerator	Lag 0	-12.084	2.546	-4.746	0.000
WSpeed	Delay		6			
	Numerator	Lag 0	0.178	0.081	2.209	0.027
Humidity	Delay		4			
	Numerator	Lag 0	7.893	3.272	2.412	0.016
Precip	Delay		1			
	Numerator	Lag 0	0.316	0.109	2.908	0.004
Pressure	Delay		8			
	Numerator	Lag 0	0.254	0.064	3.972	0.000

The analysis of fit statistics and prediction accuracy for the *ARIMA/TF mode*l yielded a small coefficient of determination, R^2=0.281. But the goal here is to correct the errors in the *RF model* and obtain a hybrid model that adequately approximates the original data.

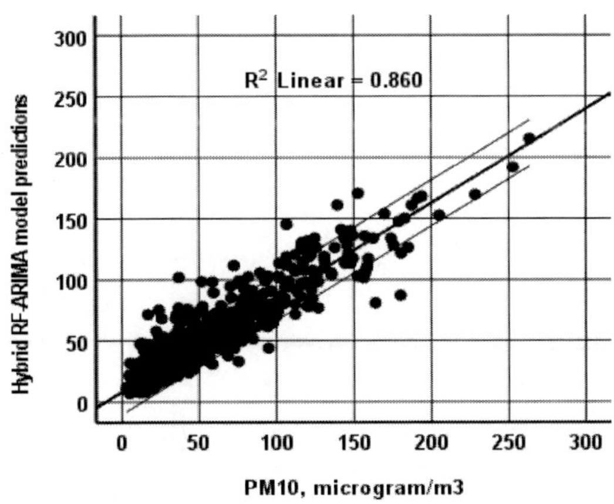

Figure 6.5. Predicted values from the hybrid *RF_ARIMA* model against the PM_{10} measured values for the city of Haskovo with a 95% confidence interval.

Finally, applying formulas (6.1), the hybrid model and its residuals were obtained. Model statistics are given in the third row of Table 6.2. Figure 6.5 presents the predicted values against $pm10$. Although there is no significant increase in the coefficient of determination within 3%, this figure clearly shows that the hybrid model predicts the highest PM_{10} values, reaching maximum values of about $220\ \mu g/m^3$ against the measured maximum values within $250 - 264\ \mu g/m^3$.

The ACF in Figure 6.6 shows there is no autocorrelation in the final hybrid model. Therefore, we can assume that this model is statistically adequate.

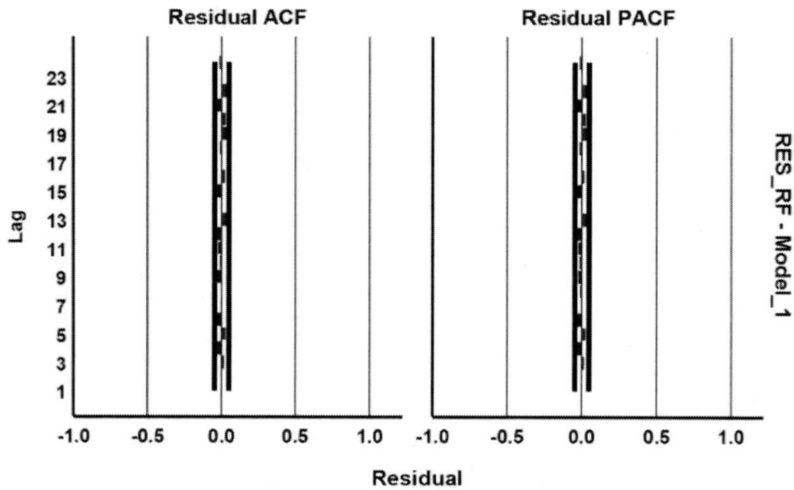

Figure 6.6. ACF and PACF of the final hybrid *RF_ARIMA* error model of PM_{10} for the city of Haskovo.

Conclusion

This case study develops an efficient methodology for constructing a hybrid method based on RF and Box-Jenkins ARIMA methods for more accurately predicting air pollution data, depending on the effects of meteorological and atmospheric variables. The approach was demonstrated for modeling empirical data on PM_{10} concentrations in the city of Haskovo, Bulgaria. RF error correction resulted in a model with better statistics, explaining 86% of the modeled data and accurately predicting high PM_{10} levels.

The proposed methodology can also be used for modeling other types of time series across different fields of application.

References

[1] Breiman, L., 2001. Random forests. *Machine Learning*, 45(1), pp. 5-32.
[2] Box, G. E. P., Jenkins, G. M., Reinsel, G. S., Ljung, G. M., 2016. *Time Series Analysis, Forecasting and Control, 5th edn.*, John Wiley & Sons. Inc, New Jersey.
[3] Gocheva-Ilieva, S., Ivanov, A., Stoimenova-Minova, M. Prediction of PM10 air pollution using random forests with ARIMA error correction, in *19th Conference on Applied Mathematics (APLIMAT 2020),* 4-6 February 2020, Bratislava, Slovakia, Aplimat Conference Proceedings, D. Szarková, D. Richtáriková, M. Prášilová (eds.), Slovak University of Technology in Bratislava, Bratislava, 2020, pp. 537–545.
[4] Salford Predictive Modeler (SPM). https://www.minitab.com/en-us/products/spm/.
[5] EU air quality standards, 2024. https://environment.ec.europa.eu/topics/air/air-quality/eu-air-quality-standards_en.

Chapter 7

Temporal-Causal Approach for Air Pollution Forecasting

Abstract

High levels of air pollution are dangerous to human health, which is a current problem for densely populated cities worldwide. Studying this problem can help detect pollutants' time dependencies on basic meteorological measurements and other factors for future prediction and elaborate corresponding alarms when official upper pollution limits are exceeded. In this case study, temporal-causal models (TCM) based on previous daily time observations and meteorological measurements in the city of Plovdiv, Bulgaria, are applied. Vector-type temporal-causal models are constructed and analyzed for carbon dioxide (CO_2), nitrogen dioxide (NO_2), sulfur dioxide (SO_2), and fine dust particles below sizes 10, 2.5, and 1 micron (PM_{10}, $PM_{2.5}$, and PM_1), respectively. Pollution concentrations are predicted seven days ahead.

Keywords: Ganger causality, impact diagram, nitrogen dioxide, sulfur dioxide, temporal causal model, system model

7.1. Introduction

The purpose of this case study is to investigate the mutual relationships between the main air pollutants using vector-type temporal-causal analysis. Modeling is conducted with empirical data for nitrogen dioxide (NO_2), sulfur dioxide (SO_2), carbon dioxide (CO_2), and particulate matter (PM) with sizes under 10, 2.5, and 1 micron (PM_{10}, $PM_{2.5}$, and PM_1), and meteorological factors. The goal is to identify the causal relationships between these pollutants, to identify the problematic pollutants, as well as to demonstrate the possibilities for evaluating short-term forecasts for future pollution. The approach is used for local data for the North-western part of the city of Plovdiv, Bulgaria. But in the same way, it can easily be applied to any urban area, both locally and on a much more general scale, depending on the available data.

The TCM is based on Granger causality [1]. The method and the relevant literature sources are given in Chapter 3.

Statistical analyses in this case study were carried out using the TCM engine of the IBM SPSS Statistics [2].

7.2. Study Area and Data Description

The following is the description of the selected location and modeling data.

- Study area: Plovdiv

Considered the oldest continuously inhabited city in Europe, Plovdiv, Bulgaria has a history and prehistory that dates back 8000 years [3]. Nowadays, Plovdiv is the second-largest city in Bulgaria. It is located in the Upper Thracian valley, on both banks of the Maritsa River, on six syenite hills. It has a population of over 360,000 as of 2023 in the greater metropolitan area. The climate is transitional-continental with an average annual temperature of 12.3°C. During the summer months, the average maximum temperatures are within 30-31°C, with maximum daily temperatures over 40 and 42°C also being reached. The average annual minimum temperature is 6.5°C. In Plovdiv, weak winds prevail (0 - 5 m/s), with winds up to 1 m/s being up to 95% during the year [4].

- Data

We examine average daily data for six air pollutants, namely NO_2, SO_2, CO_2, PM_{10}, $PM_{2.5}$, and PM_1, collected by an Alphasense automatic monitoring station with optical sensors. The station is located on the roof of Plovdiv University, the New building. The period of collected data is from 11 April 2021 to 24 March 2023. The main descriptive statistics of the pollutants' time series are given in Table 7.1.

In Plovdiv, the low temperatures in the winter months help to retain harmful emissions in the air. Other conditions for increased levels of air pollutants are intensive car traffic, various combustion processes from household and industry, road maintenance, and others in the Plovdiv District.

In particular, NO_2 and SO_2 mainly result from the combustion of fossil fuels, coal at power plants, and automobile traffic.

Table 7.1. Descriptive statistics of the air pollutants' variables used for temporal causal modeling for Plovdiv

Statistic	NO_2 (ppm)	SO_2 (ppm)	CO_2 (ppm)	PM_{10} (ppm)	$PM_{2.5}$ (ppm)	PM_1 (ppm)
N	713	713	713	713	713	713
Mean	0.383	0.420	196.35	28.09	9.39	5.87
Std. Dev.	0.102	0.018	93.61	109.33	15.34	7.50
Variance	0.010	0.0003	8763.42	11953.8	235.60	56.26
Minimum	0.191	0.386	2.89	0.68	0.68	0.51
Maximum	0.565	0.476	366.30	1434.86	174.97	62.15

From Table 7.1, it can be seen that for the studied period, the average 24-hour concentration of NO_2 particles is 0.383 (ppm), equal to $741\ \mu g/m^3$. This value exceeds the permissible daily limit of Bulgaria and the European Union, as well as that of the WHO of $120\ \mu g/m^3$=0.062 (ppm) about 6 times. Also, Table 7.1 shows an average daily SO_2 concentration of $1117.3\ \mu g/m^3$. This exceeds the prescribed average daily limit of $125\ \mu g/m^3$=0.047 (ppm) by more than 8.9 times. We will consider these two pollutants problematic for the given area of Plovdiv. In addition to pollutants, the monitoring station also measures the following meteorological time series: *Temperature* (°C), *Humidity* (%), *Pressure* (Pa), and *Luminosity* (watts). They are also included in the constructed models.

- Statistical measures of model performance

The quality of constructed TCM models was evaluated by the following standard statistical measures: root mean square error (RMSE), mean absolute percentage error (MAPE), and coefficient of determination (R^2), given by the expressions (2.12) - (2.15), and the root mean squared percent error (RMSPE), calculated by

$$\text{RMSPE} = 100\sqrt{\frac{1}{N}\sum_{t=1}^{N}\left(\frac{Y_t-\hat{Y}_t}{Y_t}\right)^2}, \tag{7.1}$$

where Y_t are the observed values, $\hat{Y}_t$ are the values predicted by the model at time t, N is the sample size. We consider that models perform better when the coefficient of determination is close to 1, and the error measures are small.

Model selection with multiple nested valid models was performed by using the Akaike information criterion (AIC) and Schwarz's Bayesian information criterion (BIC), where the minimum value of any of these criteria is selected [5, 6].

Along with these measures, the reliability of the time series models was assessed by examining their residuals, which should also be small.

7.3. Initial Data Processing and Checking the TCMAssumptions

To conduct a TCM analysis, we have six time series of pollutants from Table 7.1 and four meteorological variables. Before moving on to building the models, we conducted their initial processing.

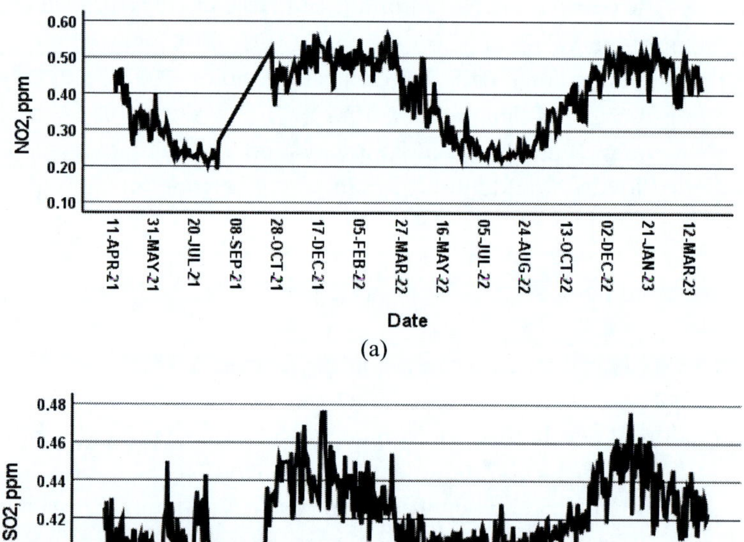

(a)

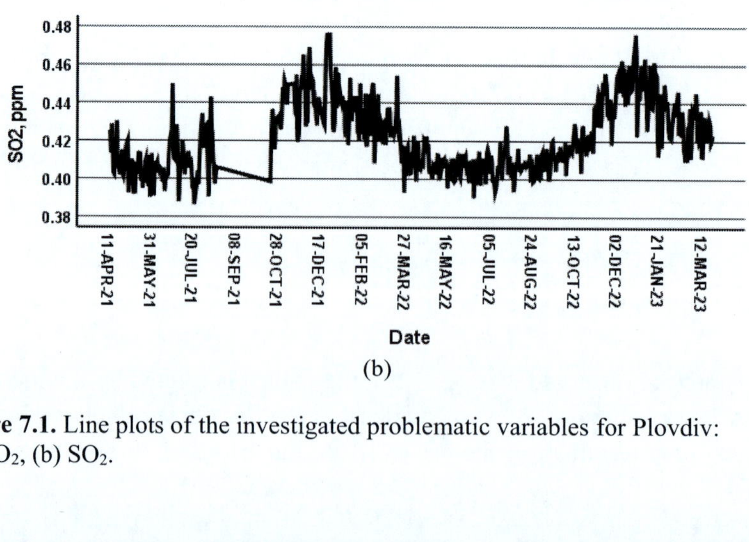

(b)

Figure 7.1. Line plots of the investigated problematic variables for Plovdiv: (a) NO_2, (b) SO_2.

The size of the data samples is N=713. Building autoregressive models does not allow for missing data [7, 8]. In our case, the original raw data had less than 15% missing values, which were replaced using the linear interpolation method.

Then the sequence plots of the variables are represented. In this study, the main results for variables *NO2* and *SO2*, corresponding to NO_2 and SO_2 pollutants, were obtained. Their line plots are shown in Figure 7.1. From Figure 7.1, it can be concluded that these time series do not contain trends. Furthermore, their ACFs and partial ACFs were graphically investigated. In the same way, the remaining variables were examined, and no trends were established. We can conclude that all variables are stationary. In the general case, if some of the variables have a trend, then the trend should be removed, for example, by differentiating it (once or repeatedly) to obtain a stationary time series. Stationarity is a condition for applying TCM.

Figure 7.1 shows a clear annual cyclic recurrence. During the winter periods, the values of *NO2* and *SO2* are the greatest, while during the summer months, low values are observed. From this, it can be concluded that the influence of weather conditions is significant. In the studied time period, the amplitudes for both variables exhibit similar behavior.

7.4. Results from the TCM

In this section, we present the causal relations obtained by applying the TCM method [9]. The terms "causal" and "causality" refer to Granger causality as it was described in detail in Chapter 3. Since TCM typically involves building models for multiple related time series, the result is referred to as a model system.

7.4.1. Building the TCM System Model

To build TCM models, we use data for N = 713 days described in section 7.2. For model validation and forecasting, the data for the next 7 days, chronologically after these 713, were used as out of data sample to $N1 = 720$.

Our model system includes all ten variables for the time series of the six pollutants and the four meteorological variables. Each of these variables can be a target, and all the others serve as predictors. Since the system is of autoregressive type, an important parameter is the maximum number of lags that consider the influence of the time series back from the current moment t. In the built models, we have chosen a maximum number of lags equal to 7 days. In formula (3.26), this corresponds to $q = 7$. The causal relations between variables are calculated on the basis of correlations, and their statistical significance is reported. In the resulting TCM system, only those variables remain that have statistically significant coefficients at a given level α. We apply the case $\alpha = 0.05$ as an upper significance limit.

Figure 7.2 shows the resulting TCM system of all causal relations between all ten variables. The arrows in the circle show the direction and strength of influence of the predictor on the target. A thicker arrow indicates a stronger effect.

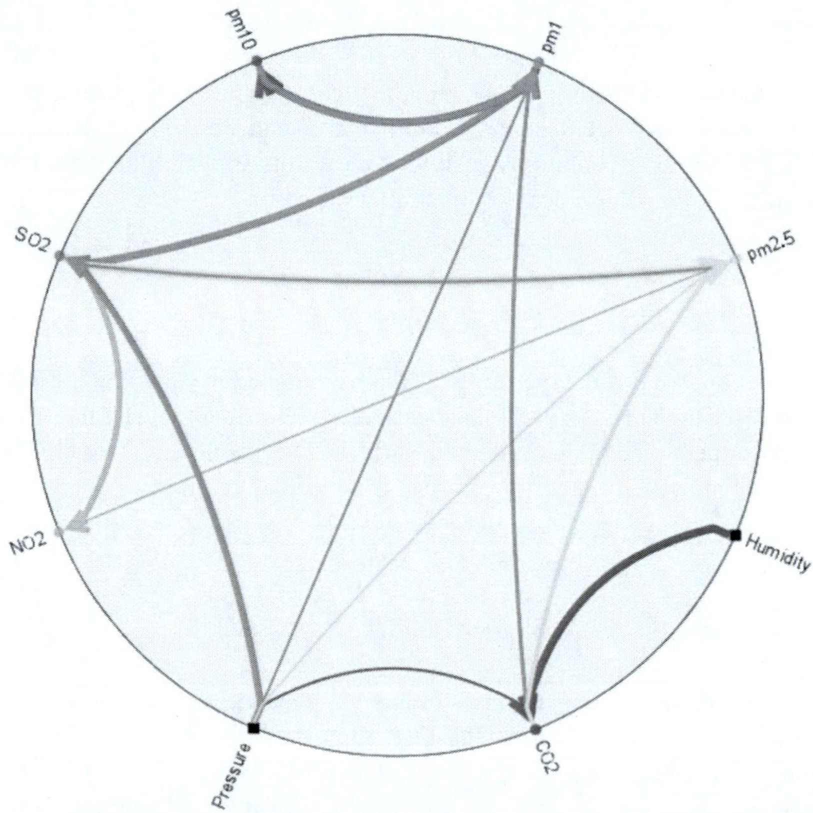

Figure 7.2. Graphical representation of the Granger causality relations between the time series in the TCM model system for Plovdiv.

Figure 7.3 shows that there are only eight variables left in the model. For example, for *NO*2, the strongest causal links stem from *SO*2 and *pm*2.5. Causal links have been established for *SO*2 with *Pressure* and *pm*2.5 (fourth column). In more detail, the causal impact of the predictors on *NO*2 and *SO*2 is displayed in Figures 7.3 and 7.4, respectively. Variables that affect the targets of interest are referred to as causes. For example, Figure 7.3 shows that we have the following causal links:

- the strongest: *Pressure* → *SO*2 → *NO*2;
- weaker: *Pressure* → *SO*2 → *PM*2.5 → *NO*2 (third column from the left side), *Humidity*→ *CO*2 → *PM*2.5 → *NO*2;
- the weakest: *Luminosity* → *NO*2.

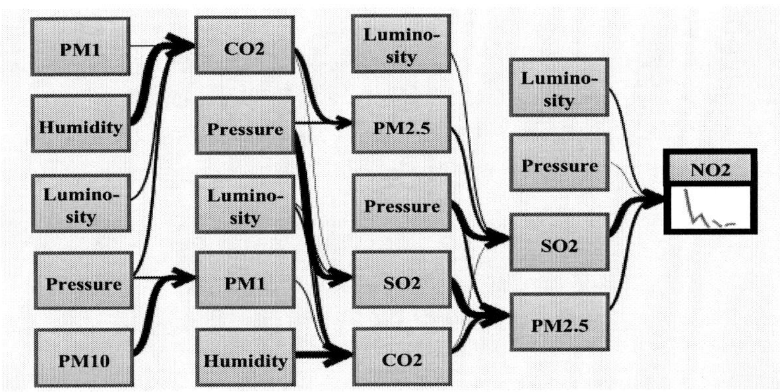

Figure 7.3. Impact diagram of causes of the time series on *NO*2.

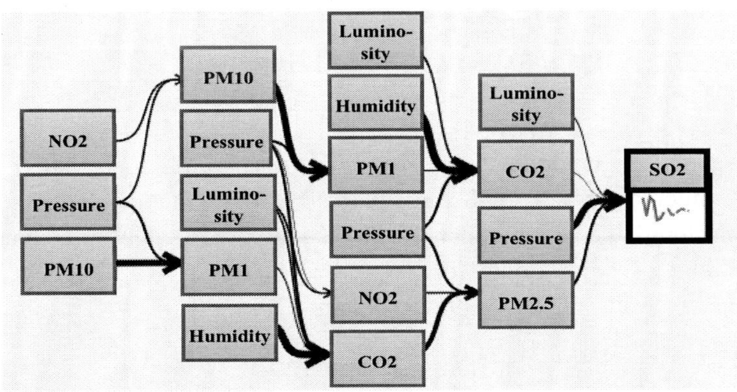

Figure 7.4. Impact diagram of causes of the time series on *SO*2.

From the impact diagram in Figure 7.4, we similarly obtain the causal relations:

- the strongest: *Pressure* → *SO2*;
- weaker: *Humidity* → *CO2* → *PM2.5* → *SO2*;
- the weakest: *Luminosity* → *SO2*.

7.4.2. Model Evaluation

The obtained statistical indicators, calculated from formulas (2.12)-(2.15) and (7.1) for the causal models generated for each of the pollutants, are given in Table 7.2. The main criterion for choosing the best model is the coefficient of determination R^2, which is the default criterion for quality evaluation of the causal models. A larger value of R^2 is assumed to correspond to a better model. Also in Table 7.2, the values of the AIC and BIC are presented, which are used for choosing the best model. It is necessary to recall that these criteria are applied to nested models, and the model with their smallest possible AIC and BIC values is selected [10].

Table 7.2. Fit statistics for the built causal models of the air pollutants variables for Plovdiv

Model target	RMSE	RMSPE	MAPE	AIC	BIC	R^2
CO2 (ppm)	12.14	0.40	0.11	3559.74	3.723.89	0.98
NO2 (ppm)	0.02	0.06	0.05	-5177.66	-5013.51	0.94
SO2 (ppm)	0.01	0.02	0.01	-6677.03	-6512.89	0.79
PM1 (ppm)	4.72	1.45	0.65	2226.96	2391.10	0.62
PM2.5 (ppm)	10.80	1.84	0.88	3395.48	3559.63	0.53
PM10 (ppm)	86.72	7.00	2.87	6336.44	6500.59	0.39

In Table 7.2, the models are arranged in descending order relative to R^2. The best model with $R^2 = 0.98$ was obtained for *CO2*, i.e., it explains about 98% of the data. The next model is for *NO2*, which fits the measured data with 94%, followed by the model for *SO2*, with a fit of 79%. The lowest and unsatisfactory result of $R^2 = 0.39$ was obtained for *PM10*.

7.4.3. Predictive Performance of the Models

The quality of fit of the *NO*2 and *SO*2 models to the measured data is depicted in Figures 7.5a and b, respectively. The figures show a good concordance between the model-predicted values and the measured ones, for *NO*2 with 94% and for *SO*2 with 79%.

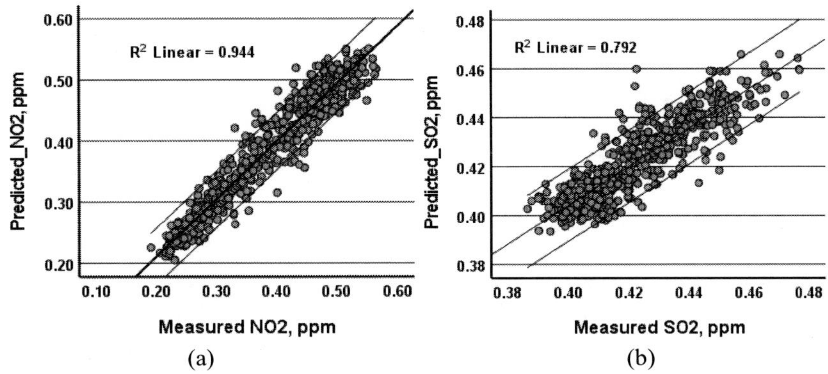

Figure 7.5. Observed and predicted values for: (a) *NO*2, (b) *SO*2.

7.4.4. An Analysis of Model Residuals

The quality of the constructed models and their adequacy can be verified by the behavior of their residuals $\varepsilon_t = Y_t - \hat{Y}_t$. The statistics of the normalized residuals for the constructed *NO*2 and *SO*2 TCM models are presented in Table 7.3. The respective means and medians are zero, and the skewness and kurtosis are relatively small. We can consider the residuals of both the *NO*2 and *SO*2 variables to be stationary and approximately normally distributed.

Also, visual inspection for normality of the distribution of residuals was performed by constructing their histograms [11, 13]. Figure 7.6 illustrates the histograms of the normalized residuals of the *NO*2 and *SO*2 models, respectively.

The results shown in Table 7.3 and Figure 7.6 suggest that the residuals are normally distributed.

Additionally, Figure 7.7 shows the normalized residual ACF of the built TCM models of the *NO*2 and *SO*2 time series. No large deviations of the ACF coefficients outside the confidence intervals are observed. Also, all Ljung-Box statistics are insignificant at the 0.05 level. It can be concluded that the models exhibit no autocorrelation, are adequate, and suitable for forecasting [11-13].

Table 7.3. Statistics of the normalized residuals of the built causal models of the time series *NO*2 and *SO*2 for Plovdiv

Statistic	*NResidual_NO*2	*NResidual_SO*2
N valid	706	706
N missing	7	7
Mean	0.0000	0.0000
Median	0.0005	-0.0006
Std. Deviation	0.0243	0.0084
Variance	0.001	0.000
Skewness	0.045	0.107
Kurtosis	1.171	1.231
Minimum	-0.09	-0.04
Maximum	0.09	0.03

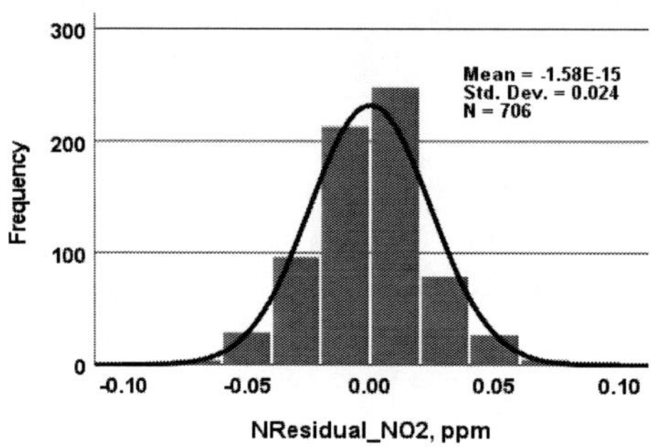

(a)

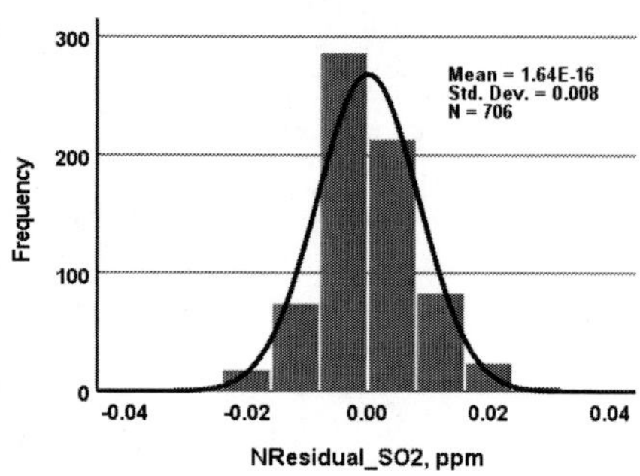

(b)

Figure 7.6. Histograms of the normalized residuals for: (a) *NO*2 and (b) *SO*2 models.

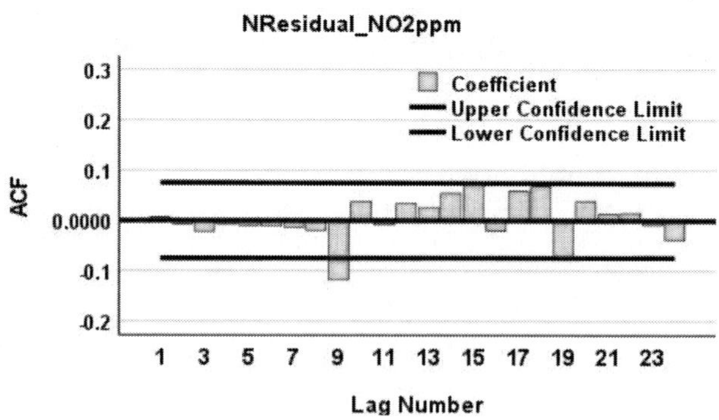

(a)

Figure 7.7. (Continued).

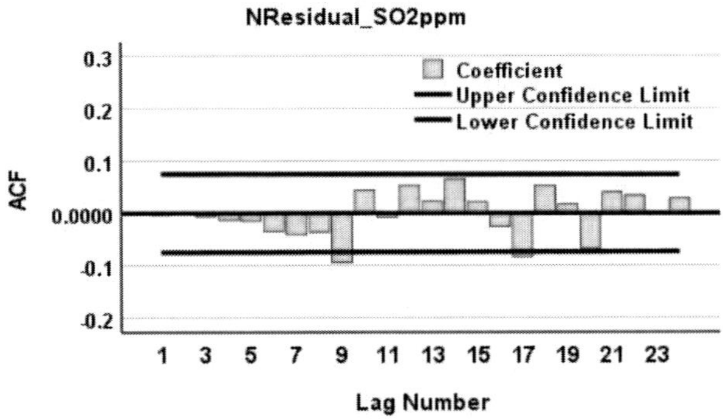

(b)

Figure 7.7. Residual ACF plots for problematic variables: (a) *NO*2, (b) *SO*2.

7.5. The Application of TCM Models to Forecast the Out-of-Data Sample

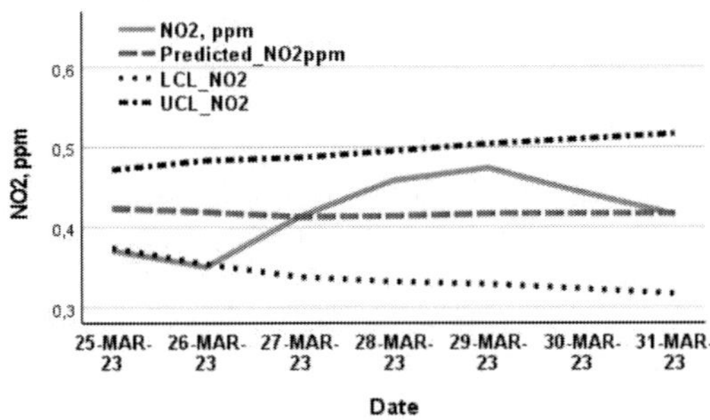

(a)

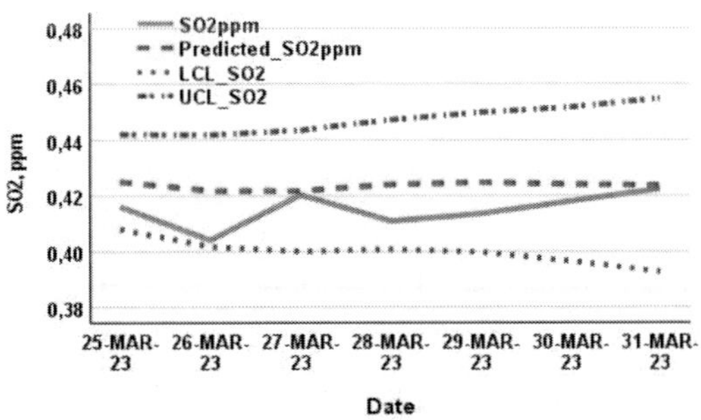

(b)

Figure 7.8. Forecasting for 7 days ahead with lower and upper 95% confidence limits for: (a) *NO*2, (b) *SO*2.

Verification of the models was performed to predict the values of the variables 7 days after the last day used in the modeling process. Figure 7.8 presents the forecasted values of *NO*2 and *SO*2 against those measured with lower and upper limits of confidence levels. To obtain these values, all of the predictors are forecasted in the built TCM model from the previous subsection 7.4. Good forecasts are observed for both pollutants.

Conclusion

In this chapter, the average daily measurements of six pollutants (NO_2, SO_2, CO_2, PM_{10}, $PM_{2.5}$, and PM_1) and four meteorological variables (Temperature, Pressure, Humidity, and Luminosity) in the city of Plovdiv, Bulgaria, were modeled. The studied period was from 11th April 2021 to 24th March 2023, or 713 days. The pollutants NO_2 and CO_2 were found to be more problematic than others. They exceed the national and European daily average permissible limits by 6 and 8.9 times, respectively. Using the temporal causal modeling (TCM) approach, Granger causal relationships between the air pollutants were revealed. The overall TCM system vector type model was built. Using the resulting impact diagrams, the strength of the relationships between the pollutants was determined. The highest results achieved according to the coefficient of determination are: model fit of 98% for CO_2, 94% for NO_2, and 79% for SO_2. The TCM system model was applied to predict all the variables included in it. Seven-day forecasts were generated.

We can conclude that TCM provides a convenient and efficient vector method for simultaneously studying and modeling causal relationships among multiple variables, as well as for forecasting time series in the field of air pollution.

References

[1] Granger, C. W., 1969. Investigating causal relations by econometric models and cross-spectral methods. *Econometrica: Journal of the Econometric Society*, 37(3), pp. 424-438.

[2] IBM SPSS Statistics, https://www.ibm.com/products/spss-statistics.

[3] Plovdiv: Europe's Oldest Continuously Inhabited City, https://www.thecollector.com/plovdiv-history-prehistory/.

[4] Plovdiv. https://en.wikipedia.org/wiki/Plovdiv

[5] Akaike, H., 1974. A new look at the statistical model identification. *IEEE Transactions on Automatic Control*, 19(6), 716-723.

[6] Schwarz, G., 1978. Estimating the dimension of a model. *Annals of Statistics,* 6, pp. 461-464.

[7] Box, G. E. P., Jenkins, G. M., Reinsel, G. S., Ljung, G. M., 2016. *Time Series Analysis, Forecasting and Control, 5th edn*., John Wiley & Sons. Inc, New Jersey.

[8] Pankratz, A., 1991. *Forecasting with Dynamic Regression Models*. John Wiley & Sons, New York.

[9] Ivanov, A. V., Gocheva-Ilieva, S. G., Stoimenova-Minova, M. P., *Temporal-causal modeling of air pollution in the city of Plovdiv*, Bulgaria: a case study, J. Phys.: Conf. Ser., Vol. 2675, 012002, 2023, IOP.

[10] Magnus Y. R., Katishev, P. K. and Peresetsij, A. A., 2007. *Econometrics. An introductory course. 8th ed.,* Moscow, Delo, (in Russian).

[11] Gocheva-Ilieva, S., Voynikova, D., Stoimenova, M., Ivanov, A. and Iliev, I., 2019. Regression trees modeling of time series for air pollution analysis and forecasting. *Neural Computing and Applications*, 31(12), pp. 9023-9039.

[12] Livieris, I., Stavroyiannis, S., Pintelas, E. and Pintelas, P., 2020 A novel validation framework to enhance deep learning models in time-series forecasting. *Neural Computing and Applications*. 32(23), pp. 17149-17167.

[13] Brockwell, P. J. and Davis, R. A., 2016. *Introduction to time series and forecasting*. Berlin, Springer.

Chapter 8

Stacked Discrete Wavelet Transform and Ensemble Learning for NO_2 and SO_2 Prediction

Abstract

This Chapter presents a new approach for statistical modeling of time series data of air pollutants, depending on meteorological factors. A new framework based on the discrete wavelet transform (DWT) is proposed for decomposing the pollutant's time series as a sum of components that represent trend, seasonality, and other specific characteristics of the studied variables. A key element in the applied DWT is an adaptive scheme for selecting the threshold value to control the reverse DWT's accuracy for achieving better prediction of the original time series. The resulting components are modeled with cutting-edge predictive ensemble tree algorithms, including bagging, boosting, and stacking techniques. This approach is tested with daily averaged data measured with a mobile automated station in the city of Plovdiv, Bulgaria. All models are analyzed, evaluated, and cross-validated. The models are applied to short-term pollution forecasts for seven days ahead. Each individual model is calculated in 1-2 seconds on a regular Windows PC or laptop.

Keywords: air pollutant, bagging, boosting, discrete wavelet transform, ensemble learning, forecasting, time series, stacking, threshold

8.1. Introduction

In our century, huge amounts of data are constantly accumulating from various sources - from measurements in production processes and practices, sensors, the Internet, space stations, and others. Much of this data is or can easily be represented as a time series. The availability of data from measurements in the environment, and in particular for air pollutants, makes it possible to process and analyze, and above all, to predict the future state of air cleanliness. The task can be for a local or global area. In particular, the levels of air pollutants depend on many different factors. Meteorological conditions are particularly important for the formation and transport of aerosols in the air. They are rapidly changing and interacting with each other and cannot be ignored [1, 2]. Therefore, mathematical and statistical modelling of this type of data is an important and non-trivial task to provide reliable tools for air quality research and prediction.

Nitrogen dioxide (NO_2) and Sulphur dioxide (SO_2) are among the main harmful pollutants in urban air, and their elevated concentrations are a constant problem in many countries worldwide. Like other aerosols in the air, NO_2 and SO_2 levels depend on many factors, including rapidly changing weather and atmospheric conditions. A more detailed description of these two pollutants and a literature review of research on them are presented in Chapter 1. The problematic high levels of both pollutants, NO_2 and SO_2, are in the summer months, while in the winter they are at their lowest. It follows that the influence of air temperature, humidity, air pressure, and luminosity has a significant relationship with pollutant levels.

In this chapter, a new methodology and framework for time series analysis is proposed, based on combinations of DWT and different ensemble tree ML approaches. The goal is to remove noise from the data by adaptive selection and combination of wavelets, then construct predictive regression models with ensemble methods with increased performance and high prediction ability.

The developed approach is applied to the analysis and prediction of air pollutants NO_2 and SO_2, depending on four meteorological variables. Models are selected and evaluated using standard statistical indicators. In addition, a diagnosis of the residuals of the models is carried out to check their adequacy. Models are validated by applying them for short-term predictions to data not used in their construction [3].

8.2. Framework of the Study

For modeling a given time series *Y* (i.e., NO_2 or SO_2), we propose the following framework:

1) The initial dataset *Y*, where *Y*=*NO*2 or *Y*=*SO*2, is divided into two parts: training dataset and validation dataset.
2) The training dataset is denoised adaptively using the discrete wavelet transform (DWT). DWT is applied with three families of mother

wavelets – biorthogonal splines (B), Daubechies (D), and Haar wavelets (H), denoted by $w_p, p = 1,2,3$ for B, D, H, respectively.

3) The denoised samples are averaged to achieve a more reliable model (wY).
4) Three base ensemble tree models are built using available predictors for all data.
5) A stacked model is calculated by averaging the selected base models.
6) Applying the stacked model for the short-term forecast of *Y* on the validation dataset.

For the construction of the three base regression type models, the following ensemble machine learning methods are used: Random Forests [4, 5], CART Ensemble and Bagging [6], and Adaptively resampling and combine (Arcing) [7]. Their algorithms and features are described in Chapter 3. Stacked regressions are studied in [8]. More on these ensemble methods and their applications can be found in [9-12] and the literature cited therein.

Statistical analyses are performed using the authors' codes in Wolfram Mathematica [13] for DWT, Salford Predictive Modeler (SPM) [14] for ensemble learning models, and SPSS software [15].

8.3. Study Area and Data

We will demonstrate the proposed framework for data modeling of two air pollutants – NO_2 and SO_2 in the city of Plovdiv, Bulgaria. The study area, time period, and data have already been used and partially described in Chapter 7. The four meteorological time series used as predictors in the models are: air temperature, relative humidity, air pressure, and luminosity. In this Chapter, we denote the used relevant variables by *NO2*, *SO2*, *Temp*, *Hum*, *Press*, and *Lum*, respectively.

To conduct the analyses, we divide all available N1=720 data into two parts. The first part for N = 713 days is used as a learning set, and the measurements for the next 7 days are used for an independent out-of-sample test. The latter is designed validate the models and evaluate their forecasts. The initial raw data had fewer than 15% missing values. They were replaced by the average known values for the same dates measured in subsequent years. This method of handling missing values differs from the linear interpolation in Chapter 7 but does not significantly change the statistical indicators of the variables compared to Table 7.1.

Descriptive statistics of the obtained all-time series for *N*=713 days are shown in Table 8.1. Table 8.1 shows that pollutant levels both for NO_2 and SO_2 are problematic. The permissible average daily concentrations for the European Union, Bulgaria, as well as for the WHO for NO_2 and SO_2, are $120\ \mu g/m^3$ = 0.062 ppm and $125\ \mu g/m^3$ = 0.047 ppm, respectively [16]. An excess of about 6 times was observed for NO_2 and 9 times for SO_2.

Table 8.1. Descriptive statistics of the used variables

Variable	Statistics				
	Mean	Std. Dev.	Variance	Min	Max
NO2, ppm	0.383	0.102	0.01	0.191	0.565
SO2, ppm	0.420	0.018	0.0003	0.386	0.476
Temp, °C	16.24	9.31	86.65	-3.03	35.29
Hum, %	59.40	19.26	370.89	22.16	100.00
Press, Pa	995.83	6.91	47.73	975.46	1018.10
Lum, watts	3873	1719	2955626	176	7652

Sequence plots of the pollutant's variables are shown in Figure 8.1. The problematic high levels of both pollutants, NO_2 and SO_2, are in the summer months, while in the winter they are at their lowest. It follows that air temperature, humidity, air pressure, and luminosity have a significant relationship with pollutant levels.

8.4. Denoising the Time Series Using the Discrete Wavelet Transform

We conduct the modeling and analyses according to the proposed methodology and framework.

8.4.1. Adaptive Wavelet Denoising

First, we will use the training sample with *N*=713 observations for denoising with three different families of wavelets – biorthogonal splines (B), Daubechies (D), and Haar wavelets (H). The decomposition of a given time series in DWT is carried out by calculating its coefficients in the stage of extracting the refinements. A short theoretical basis on this procedure is presented in Chapter 3. After performing a chosen DWT, an inverse transform is applied to recover the original data. In this step, the main element is to set the appropriate threshold value to achieve the desired accuracy of the extracted waveform. We denote the threshold by *th* (see also Chapter 3, paragraph 3.2).

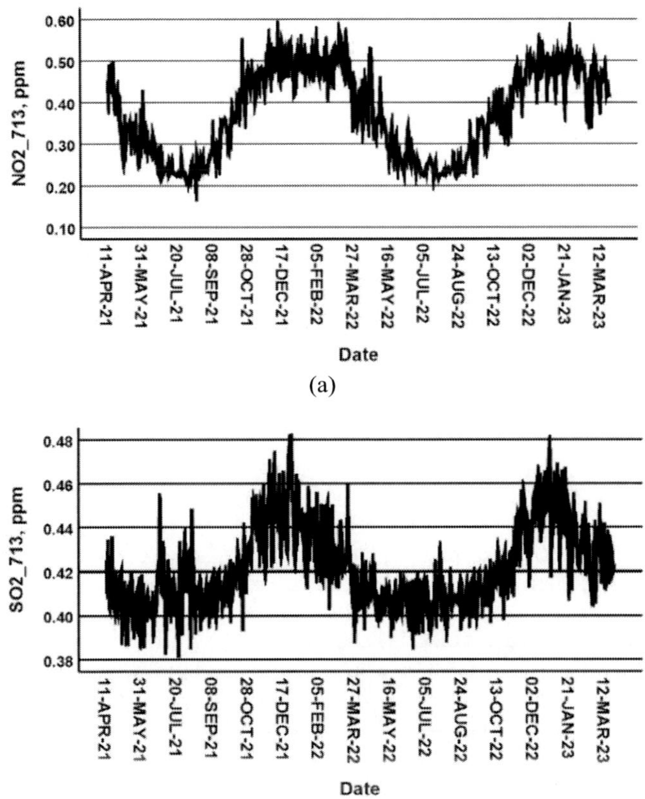

(b)

Figure 8.1. Sequence plots of the dependent variables: (a) *NO*2, (b) *SO*2.

In this study, we have used a simple adaptive approach to select the threshold value *th*. This is done by comparing the result with the ACF of the residuals of the constructed wavelet model and choosing *th* so that the coefficients of the ACF coefficients of the residuals are within the confidence intervals. For our data, good results were obtained at values *th*=*std*, *std*/2, *std*/3, and *std*/4, where *std* is the standard deviation of the original time series. We denote the selected wavelet models (w-models) for *NO*2 at *th*=*std*/3 by

B_NO2, *D_NO2*, and *H_NO2*, respectively, for B, D, and H DWT. Similarly, the DWT models of *SO2* at *th=std*/4 are denoted by *B_SO2*, *D_SO2*, and *H_SO2*.

The approximations obtained after the inverse DWT for both pollutants are very good and within the limits of the ACF of their residuals. The corresponding statistical measures and results from the Durbin-Watson (D-W) statistics of these models are given in the upper rows of Table 8.2. D-W is calculated by regression of a given model with the target *Y*. It is seen that the D-W statistics are close to 2, so we would conclude that there is no serial correlation in the models' residuals.

Table 8.2. Performance statistics of all built models in Chapter 8

Model	Statistics				
	Sample size	RMSE	MAPE	R^2	D-W
B_NO2	713	0.0139	3.08	0.982	1.875
D_NO2	713	0.0144	3.17	0.981	1.760
H_NO2	713	0.0132	2.95	0.984	1.914
B_SO2	713	0.0022	0.40	0.985	2.329
D_SO2	713	0.0017	0.30	0.991	2.321
H_SO2	713	0.0018	0.33	0.990	2.176
wNO2	713	0.0106	2.36	0.990	2.055
wSO2	713	0.0013	0.24	0.995	2.384
NA30	720	0.0106	2.26	0.990	2.033
NRF300	720	0.0112	2.42	0.990	1.935
NC30	720	0.0106	2.30	0.990	1.970
SA15	720	0.0042	0.74	0.945	1.889
SRF200	720	0.0041	0.73	0.943	1.791
SC40	720	0.0040	0.70	0.952	1.854
S_NO2	720	0.0106	2.30	0.990	2.027
S_SO2	720	0.0039	0.70	0.957	1.867

8.4.2. Averaging the DWT Models

Following the proposed methodology, we average the w-models with the expression

$$wY = \frac{B\_Y + D\_Y + H\_Y}{3}, \tag{8.1}$$

where $Y = NO2$ or $Y = SO2$. Using this linear combination, the statistics of the averaged models were found to improve over their corresponding base models, as is presented in Table 8.2.

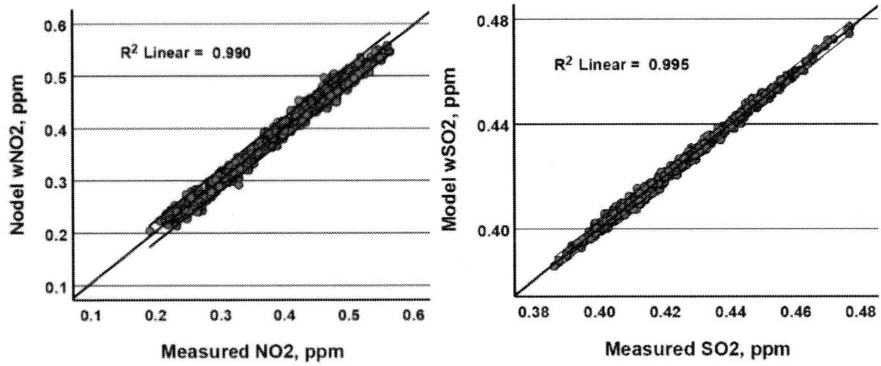

(a) (b)

Figure 8.2. Comparison between measured data and w-models for: (a) $NO2$ vs. $wNO2$, (b) $SO2$ vs. $wSO2$.

Figure 8.2 shows the quality of fitting of the w-models to the measured data. Excellent correspondence is observed. In particular, we should note that the combined w-models very well approximate the high and low values of the two time series, as can be seen from Figure 8.2.

The ACF of the residuals of the averaged w-models is shown in Figure 8.3. Also, from Table 8.2, the D-W statistics are close to 2, which indicates there is no autocorrelation in the residuals. Also, as the residuals are small and almost within the confidence intervals, we can conclude that the models are adequate.

8.5. Building the Base Models for NO_2 and SO_2

The use of DWT was intended to remove the influence of noise in the raw data. When we aim to predict future values of a time series, we need regression-type models as well as predictors whose values are known in the future. To evaluate the forecasts, we introduce the four meteorological variables described in Table 8.1, with values up to $N1$=720 observations. Model variables $wNO2$ and $wSO2$ were selected as target variables.

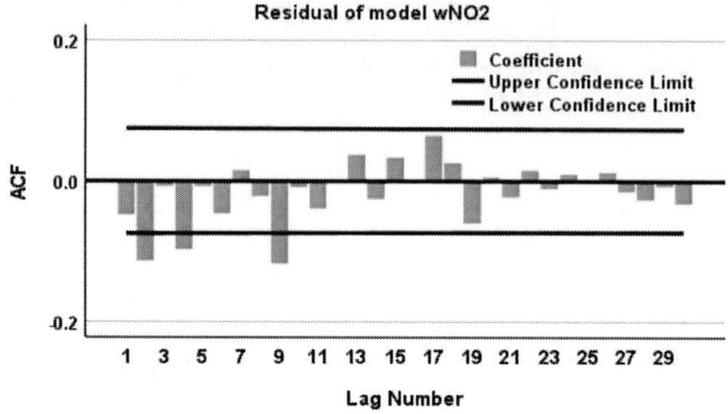

(a)

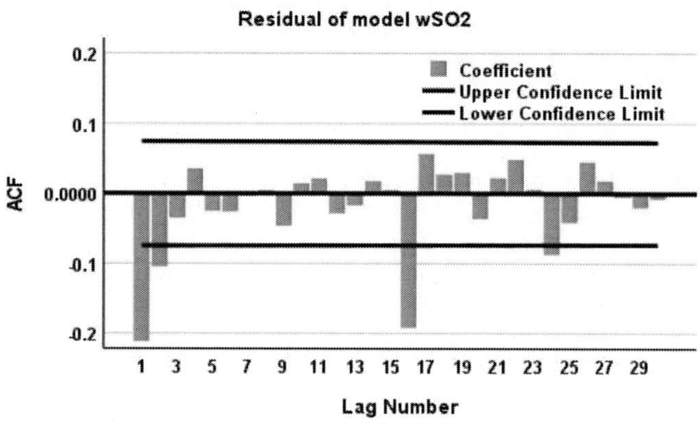

(b)

Figure 8.3. ACF of the residuals of the selected w-models for: (a) *NO*2, (b) *SO*2.

Multiple ensemble models were constructed by varying the hyperparameters as follows:

1. For RF (R): the number of trees in the ensemble was set to 100, 200, and 300; procedure for testing the models – the OOB by default; number of randomly selected predictors – 2, 3, and 4; minimum cases in terminal node – 5.
2. For Arcing (A) models: 20, 30, 40, and 50 trees in each ensemble model; m1:m2 = 10:5, 5:5; 10-fold cross-validation.
3. For CEB (C) models - as for Arcing.

All models were evaluated according to usual statistical measures (2.12)-(2.15) for all $N1 = 720$ observations. The corresponding selected best models are indicated by adding the number of trees to their name, e.g., *NR*200, *NA*30, etc. Their remaining parameters are given in Table 8.2.

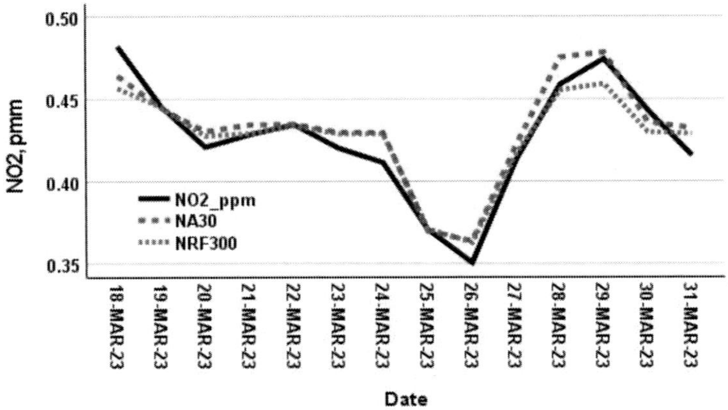

(a)

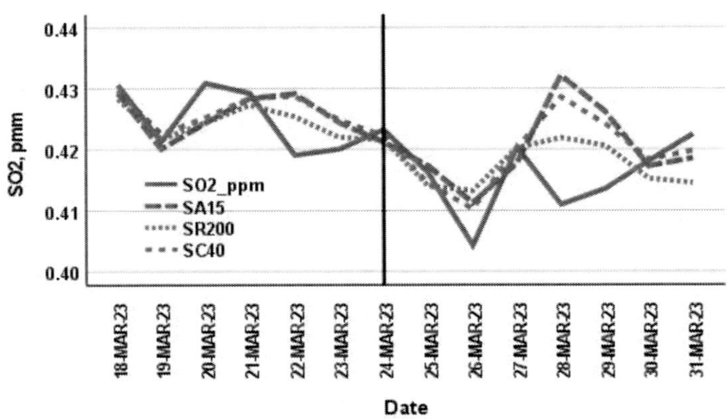

(b)

Figure 8.4. Forecasts of the selected base models for the last 14 days: to the left of the vertical line are the predictions of the last 7 days of the training sample, to the right of the vertical line are the forecasts for the test sample: (a) for *NO*2, (b) for *SO*2.

From the results in Table 8.2, it can be seen that the models are improved in stages, following the developed modeling framework. Finally, after the last step, the *S_NO*2 and *S_SO*2 models showed the best statistics. The only exception was obtained for model *NA*30, whose MAPE of 0.26 is minimal. However, when examining the ACF of the residuals, this model gives way to the stacked model *S_NO*2. The forecasts for the last 7 test days for the three best ensemble models are illustrated in Figure 8.4 along with their confidence intervals.

A relatively very good quality of the predicted values is observed. The quality of the *NO*2 forecasts is significantly better, most likely due to better statistics compared to *SO*2.

8.6. Building and Evaluating the Stacked Models

The final step of the proposed methodology is the stacking of the selected best base models from paragraph 8.5. For this purpose, we averaged the resulting base models separately for *NO*2 and *SO*2. For *NO*2, the sacked model *S_NO*2 is found by

$$S\_NO2 = \frac{NA30+NR300+NC30}{3}. \tag{8.2}$$

Analogically, we average the values of the three base models to obtain the stacked model for *SO*2, denoted by *S_SO*2

$$S\_SO2 = \frac{SA15+SR200+SC40}{3}. \tag{8.3}$$

The statistical indices of the two stacked models *S_NO*2 and *S_SO*2 are given at the bottom of Table 8.2. The comparison with the others shows that they improve the performance of all other models. For the prediction of *NO*2 with model *S_NO*2, we obtained a coefficient of determination R^2=0.990 and MAPE=2.3%. With model *S_SO*2, we have R^2=0.957, RMSE=0.0039, and MAPE=0.70, respectively. Figure 8.5 presents a scatter plot comparing the values of the stacked models with the initial variables *NO*2 and *SO*2, supplemented up to *N*1=720 observations. Very good agreement with the measured data and small deviations from the confidence intervals are observed.

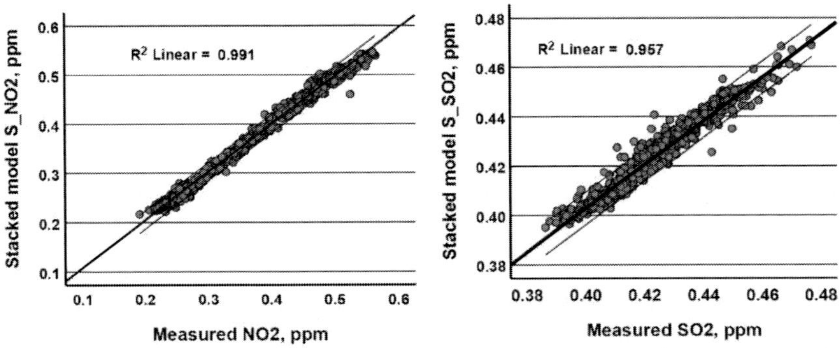

(a) (b)

Figure 8.5. Scatter plots of stacked models versus pollutants' variables: (a) for *NO*2, (b) for *SO*2.

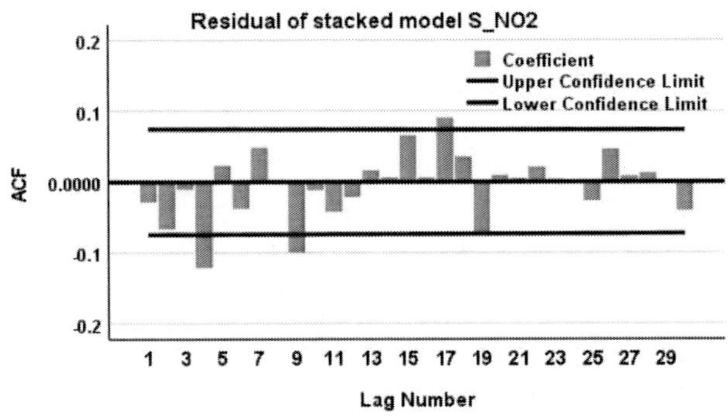

(a)

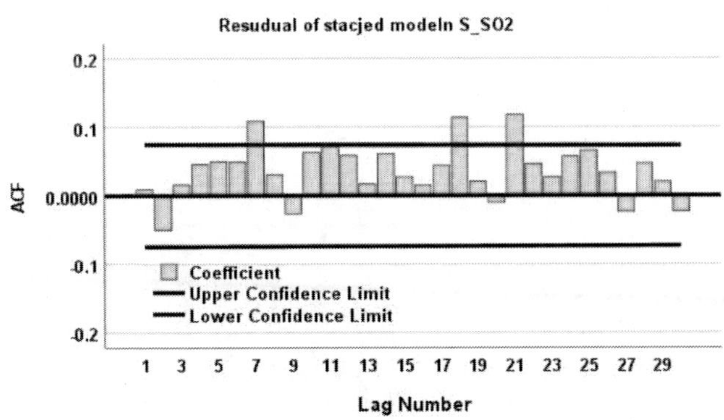

(b)

Figure 8.6. ACF plots of the residuals of the stacked models: (a) for *S_NO*2, (b) for *S_SO*2.

The ACFs of residuals of staked models with no autocorrelation are shown in Figure 8.6.

8.7. Forecasting the Test Dataset

The forecast values only for the last 7 days, saved for model validation, are shown in Figure 8.7. We can conclude that the proposed methodology and research framework are effective tools for increasing the performance of ML methods for modeling and forecasting air pollution.

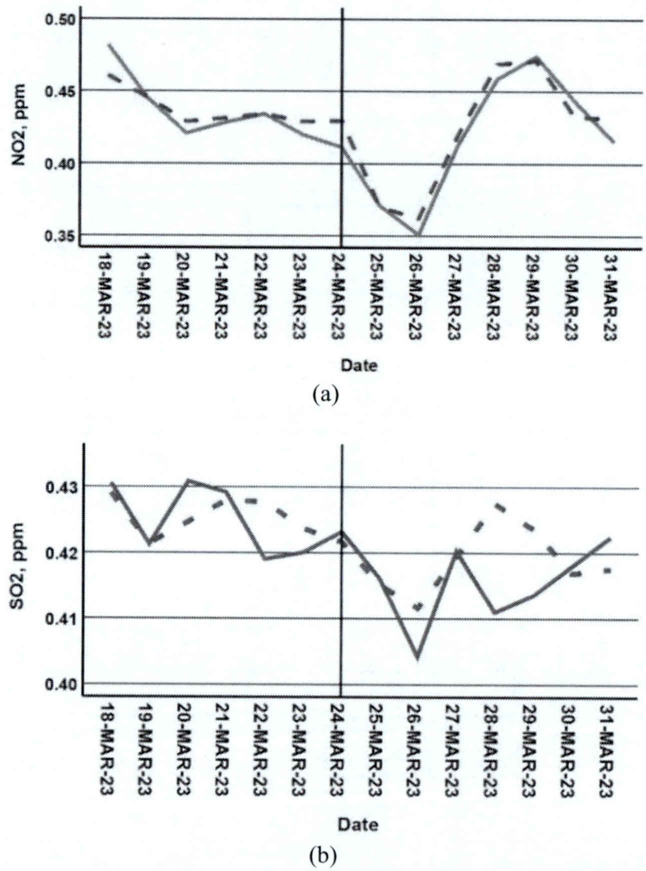

(b)

Figure 8.7. Forecasts of the stacked models for the last 14 days: to the left of the vertical line – for the last 7 days of the training sample, to the right - for the test sample: (a) for *NO*2, (b) for *SO*2.

Conclusion

In this Chapter, a general framework for time series modeling and forecasting based on wavelet analysis and tree-based ML algorithms was proposed.

The framework is applied to model two different time series - the pollutants NO_2 and SO_2. For denoising each of these initial time series, three wavelet models were constructed. After linear stacking by averaging the wavelet models for each pollutant, a corresponding w-model with improved statistical indicators was obtained. In the next step, the averaged w-models were used as targets to build regression-type models with the ML methods RF, Arcing, and CART Ensembles and Bagging, and 4 meteorological variables as predictors. The resulting models were again linearly stacked to obtain high-performance s-models. Stacked model *S_NO*2 predicts the NO_2 measurements with 99%. Accordingly, the stacked model *S_SO*2 fits SO_2 up to 96%.

The models are validated on an out-of-sample test to predict pollutant concentrations for 7 days. The resulting predictions are excellent for NO_2 and very good for SO_2.

The developed and demonstrated approach showed great ability for statistical research of complex time series from the field of environmental science.

References

[1] Seinfeld, J. and Pandis, S., 2016. *Atmospheric chemistry and physics: From air pollution to climate change, 3rd ed.* John Wiley & Sons, New Jersey, USA.

[2] Nidzgorska-Lencewicz, J., 2018. Application of artificial neural networks in the prediction of PM10 levels in the winter months: a case study in the Tricity agglomeration, Poland. *Atmosphere*, 9(6), 203.

[3] Gocheva-Ilieva, S. G., Ivanov, A. V., Stoimenova-Minova, M. P. and Koleva-Pavlova, S. K., 2023. Discrete wavelet transform and ensemble tree algorithms for air pollutant modeling: A case study. *International Journal of Membrane Science and Technology*, 10(4), 1357-1373.

[4] Breiman, L., 2001. Random forests. *Machine Learning*, 45(1), pp. 5-32.

[5] Breiman, L., and Cutler, A. 2004. *Random Forests Fortran code.* https://www.stat.berkeley.edu/~breiman/RandomForests/cc_software.htm.

[6] Breiman, L., 1996. Bagging predictors. *Machine Learning*, 24(2), pp. 123-140.

[7] Breiman, L., 1998. Arcing classifiers. *The Annals of Statistics*, 26(3), pp. 801-849.

[8] Breiman, L., 1996. Stacked regressions. *Machine Learning*, 24, pp. 49-64.

[9] Steinberg D. and Golovnya, M., 2014. Tree ensembles and extensions: An overview of treeNet, random forests, *ISLE model compression & RuleLearner*. http://info.salford-systems.com/jsm-2013-ctw2 2014.

[10] Zhou, Z. H., 2012. *Ensemble Methods: Foundations and Algorithms*. CRC Press, Boca Raton.

[11] Gocheva-Ilieva, S. G., Ivanov, A. V. and Stoimenova-Minova, M. P., 2022. Prediction of daily mean PM10 concentrations using random forest and CART ensemble and bagging stacked by MARS. *Sustainability*, 14(2), art. 798.

[12] Masih, A., 2019. Application of ensemble learning techniques to model the atmospheric concentration of SO2. *Global Journal of Environmental Science and Management*, 5(3), pp. 309-318.

[13] Wolfram Mathematica, https://www.wolfram.com/mathematica/.

[14] Salford Predictive Modeler (SPM). https://www.minitab.com/en-us/products/spm/.

[15] IBM SPSS Statistics, https://www.ibm.com/products/spss-statistics.

[16] EU air quality standards, 2024. https://environment.ec.europa.eu/topics/air/air-quality/eu-air-quality-standards_en.

About the Authors

Snezhana Georgieva Gocheva-Ilieva
Plovdiv University Paisii Hilendarski, Plovdiv, Bulgaria

Professor D.Sc. Snezhana Gocheva-Ilieva is currently a guest professor at the Faculty of Mathematics and Informatics (FMI) at Plovdiv University Paisii Hilendarski, Bulgaria. She holds a doctorate (Ph.D.) in Mathematics and Physics from Taras Shevchenko State University of Kyiv, Ukraine, since 1981. At Plovdiv University Paisii Hilendarski, she has been an Associate Professor in Computational Mathematics since 1985 and Professor of Mathematical Modeling and Application of Mathematics since 2011. She defended a thesis for a Doctor of Science degree from the FMI at the same university in 2016. Her scientific interests and achievements span machine learning, algorithms, data science, and data modeling, with applications in engineering, environmental science, materials science, and education, stochastic modeling of time series, computational statistics, analytical modeling, numerical methods, and more. Prof. Gocheva-Ilieva has published over 210 scientific papers, 2 monographs, and 15 books for students. She is the supervisor of 16 doctoral students in mathematics and computer science.

E-mail: snow@uni-plovdiv.bg.

Atanas Valev Ivanov
Plovdiv University Paisii Hilendarski, Plovdiv, Bulgaria

Associate Professor Atanas V. Ivanov received his secondary education with a specialization in Industrial Electronics at the Professional High School "Stoycho and Kitsa Marchevi" in Haskovo, Bulgaria (2005). He subsequently earned a Bachelor's degree in Mathematics (2009), a Master's degree in Applied Mathematics (2010), and a PhD in Mathematical Modelling and Applications of Mathematics (2015) from Plovdiv University Paisii Hilendarski. His doctoral dissertation, titled Statistical Modeling of Air Quality, was supervised within the Faculty of Mathematics and Informatics. Since 2023, he has been serving as an Associate Professor at the Department of Mathematical Analysis at the same university. His research interests include time series analysis, environmental statistics, air pollution modeling, machine learning applications, and statistical methods in education. He is the author of more than 30 scientific publications in peer-reviewed journals and international conference proceedings.

E-mail: aivanov@uni-plovdiv.bg.

Maya Plamenova Stoimenova-Minova
Plovdiv University Paisii Hilendarski, Plovdiv, Bulgaria

Maya Stoimenova-Minova graduated with a Bachelor's degree in Applied Mathematics from Plovdiv University Paisii Hilendarski in 2011. She then obtained a Master's degree in 2013 and a Ph.D. in 2018 at the same institution. She is currently a lecturer at the Faculty of Mathematics and Informatics of Plovdiv University. Her research focuses on the development and application of modern approaches, such as machine learning for time-series analysis and forecasting. She focuses on improving data processing methods and optimizing models to achieve greater accuracy and efficiency.

E-mail: mstoimenova@uni-plovdiv.bg.

Index

A

B

C

D

E

F

G

H

I

K

L

M

N

O

P

R

S

T

U

V

W

More books by *Snezhana Gocheva-Ilieva* can be found at:
https://novapublishers.com/writer/snezhana-gocheva-ilieva/